Memoirs of a Few

Krishna

ZORBA BOOKS

Sa tvam priyaan-priya rupaams-ca kaamaan

Abhidhyaayan naciketo 'tyasraakshiih,

Naitaam srinkam vittamayim avaapto

Yasyaam majjanti bahavo manusyaah.

I-ii-3 Kathopanishad.

Thou hast renounced all these desires and pleasurable objects of pleasant appearances, judging them by their real merits, though have not accepted this 'road of wealth' in which many mortals sink.

This memoir is dedicated to my parents, who are the reason for what I am today.

Published by Zorba Books, October 2023
Website: www.zorbabooks.com
Email: info@zorbabooks.com
Author Name: Krishna
Copyright ©: Krishna

Title: Memoirs of a Few

Printbook ISBN: 978-93-5896-830-9
Ebook ISBN: 978-93-5896-965-8

Zorba Books Pvt. Ltd. (opc)
Sushant Arcade,
Next to Courtyard Marriot,
Sushant Lok 1, Gurgaon – 122009, India

Printed by Thomson Press (India) Ltd.
B-315, Okhla Industrial Area, Phase 1, New Delhi- 110020

Contents

Contents

About the Author

N. Krishna Kumar,aka Krishna, belongs to Kerala. He retired as the Director of the Department of Mining and Geology, Kerala. After superannuating from Government service, he continued as a consultant Geologist. He was encouraged by his successful novels 'We Never Die' and 'Woes of the Princess of Conji' under the pen name Krishna, and this is his third attempt. He lives in Thiruvananthapuram, Kerala, with his wife Sarada. R.

Acknowledgement

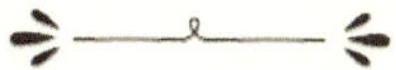

I am grateful to the Almighty for keeping me engaged in reading and writing. My gratitude to my wife for motivating me to pen down what I feel.

I am thankful to Zorba and team members for their interaction with me at each stage of the progress of the project. I thank the editor for guiding me to make the writing better. I am obliged to Zorba Publishers and those who have worked behind the screen.

Author's Note

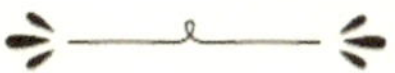

Readers may kindly note that I have recorded in the memoir some of the major events in the life of my parents and grandparents focusing on certain details only to share what I have learned from their specific life experiences.

The story of the migration of my forefathers and the number of metaphysical quotes in the memoir are those I have heard from them. Other philosophical and scriptural quotes are from my memory of reading the history and scriptures.

I have referred to Wikipedia and several published articles and they have been duly acknowledged in appropriate places. If there are any omissions, the readers may have the great heart to excuse them.

Preface

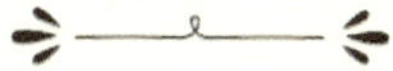

This is not an autobiography but a kind of memoir of some of my family members who were unique in their perspectives towards life and the world. Many incidents in their life have been quoted here and I have taken the liberty to introduce a few fictitious characters into their lives bringing out their exclusive personalities. Alamelu in the story has several similarities to my mother, who was never perturbed in front of debacles that struck her one after the other in life. My mother was born in a remote village in Kerala and spent her younger days in Rangoon and Quetta; her father being in the army. She started living in town after marrying my father, who was in Government service. Her great asset was that she was made of steel and despised tears as a solution to problems in life.

My father emulated the character of the British illustrated by E. M. Forster. His emotions rarely surfaced like flying fish from the deep waters. Narayana, in the story more or less simulated my father with his strong convictions. He was awfully true in his approach to life with minimum friends or no friends at all. Both my maternal and paternal great-great grandfathers' families were among the lot who migrated from Trichy in Tamil Nadu to Kerala, somewhere in the 14th century.

The scenes about forefathers are partly true and a few fictitious episodes have been sewed into the story to give a flavour to the narrations. The final retreats of Alamelu to her village and the days spent thereafter have similarities to the conviction with which my mother lived her days after the paralytic stroke left her partly immobile. My greatest wonder was that not at any time did she curse God or her fate. She bore them with fortitude and kept her wits intact until she departed from the world. Her life as well as the life I have lived so far has taught me a great lesson that, **'better it is to die while living,'** which connotes that 'stay blind to the material world before you die to know what death is.'

Keerthi

I normally walk fast, apprehending something bad might happen at the other end or something is happening where my intervention is required. But today I had reason to quicken my footsteps since my mind was on fire. I trampled on grease, slipped and fell hitting my head on the pavement. I tried to get up but lost my balance and became conscious of myself lying on the operating table in a hospital.

I was not able to open my eyes or move my limbs or hands. I heard the doctors discussing the surgical procedure for stopping the bleeding inside the head. While they were hurrying with arrangements, an apparition of a middle-aged lady lying comatose like me on the bed and that of a youngster chiding me repeatedly appeared before me, almost sucking out my soul. Suddenly, I could feel my heart giving away and thudding to a halt. That was a great relief from those nerve-wrenching scenes, and availing one of the best opportunities 'I', the very consciousness seeped out through every pore in the body.

What a relief! I thought. The scenes I had seen before escaped from my consciousness—scenes that had been bothering me in my dreams for a long time, and recently I had been taking tranquilisers suggested by a doctor to get a few hours of sleep. Now, just when I was passing out, the same characters appeared and I was unable to make out whether those characters belonged to the life I had lived and forgotten or did they denote some unrealistic scenes in my current life. While the figure of the lady on the bed stirred an emotional attachment, the young man's cry surged waves of guilt. It was devouring me. His cry had always been clear, loud and accusing, "You have made a grave mistake Honourable Judge; you have made a grave mistake. You did not take cognisance of what I said and you rushed to pronounce judgement. You will pay for this." I could see the Judge resembling me, waving his hands to the security, and the young man being dragged out of the courtroom. I had just recovered from the tormenting visions and was about to take flight into the new world when somebody called me from behind. I looked intently at the figure and was amazed to see my father Narayana.

"Son, you are back? I have been waiting for you for a while. Come on. Let us rush to your mother." He grabbed my wrist and started moving towards the car parked nearby.

I was surprised at the sight of my father **at this point** in time when I was about to merge with nature and was in a kind of trance marching dumbfounded behind him. He hurried me to the car park and when I opted to drive, he declared a big 'No', got into the driver's seat, and gestured to me to occupy the front seat. He started driving fast, tearing through the rain pounding on the windshield and the roof like small hammer beats. I could not see what lay ahead through the foggy windshield glasses and wondered how he negotiated the traffic and the potholes on the road. Since we were driving through a winding mountain road, I kept silent for fear of disturbing his concentration. While negotiating one of the curves he manoeuvred, averting a collision with the boulder that had rolled down the mount blocking half the road.

Suddenly, the scene changed in front of me. I was negotiating the curve and the car collided with the boulder and turned upside down. We were both lying in pools of blood on the seats. I heard the sound of sirens and after some time I felt somebody pulling me out through the open door. I was taken in a stretcher to the ambulance. I wanted to ask about my father but could not and I felt liberated from my body.

Scenes had switched over. My father continued to drive and after a while crashed through the gate of a rather affluent building as if no barrier existed and halted on the porch. He came out, opened the door for me, grabbed my arm and climbed the steps at the entrance. The doors were closed but we managed to move into a spacious bedroom where two nurses were sitting on either side of a figure on the bed. My father pulled me nearer to the head of the figure on the bed and cried out.

"Alamelu, your son has come. See. Come on son, hold her hand," Father was stuttering, choked with emotions.

I sat close to her head, pulled her onto my lap and called "Amma, amma." The nurses were wonderstruck to see the moving head of my mother and tried to put her back in the correct position. She got up all of a sudden, embraced the figureless form of mine and started weeping profusely. She looked at my father and reached for his hand when he gently retreated and disappeared. She was still holding me when the nurses rang the bell. Footsteps were heard outside and my grandfather barged into the room. He stood gaping at my mother who was sitting on the bed still in the pose of holding me in her hands.

"Alamelu, God is great. You have regained consciousness." My grandfather was crying like a child. My grandmother and others also came rushing to the room. My mother was sitting with eyes wide open holding me tightly and an emotional drama was playing out in the room when I felt dragged by an unknown force. I was in the hospital again. I could feel the doctors trying to resuscitate me. I wanted to run back to my mother but was losing strength and was sucked back to the body through the same pores I had chosen to escape.

I suddenly opened my eyes and tried to get up. The doctors were amazed. They tried to lay me back on the table but I cried out to be released and one of the doctors succeeded in jabbing me and putting me to sleep.

I probably got up the next day or so and not on the operating table but on a bed surrounded by doctors. I snivelled to take me to Alamelu and repeated the request quite several times. The doctor gave me another jab and put me to slumber. Before losing consciousness, I heard the doctor pronouncing that I was hallucinating.

Alamelu

Many had remarked earlier that I was a born rough and tough woman. And I wondered how a son with such a fickle mind was born to me. I seldom exposed my loving heart because they were my feelings and not for displaying to others to appreciate or depreciate. I never liked wasting time doodling with any matter. I wanted everything done at a quick pace. Though my boldness or cold feelings were frightening to my husband too, deep in his heart he liked the fact that I was confident of my ability to manage any situation without his presence or support. That emboldened him to sink into his long business trips without bothering about mundane household activities.

I had just finished my bachelor's in Psychology when my marriage was fixed.

I didn't need to work unless I wanted to pursue it as an interest. It was a merger of two affluent families with a difference. I was brought up in a village atmosphere and my husband was groomed in metropolitan air. Incidentally, our fathers had both been in military service as commissioned officers and were friends. But our families had not met much because of the frequent transfers of the fathers. One day my father called me and asked me what I thought about marriage.

"Have I become a burden on you?" I responded with irritation.

"No, child. It is my friend's son who you have known since he was a child. He has completed his MBA and is running a business house of his own. If you think you are prepared, I shall ask them to visit us. I leave it to you," he said, leaving me when I was preparing to fight with him.

I did not say a word further about it thinking that the final decision lay with me. It was a real task for my mother and her sisters to groom the little short-tempered girl picking quarrels with any and everybody for the function called 'Pon parkal'. My maternal aunts had sufficiently warned me to behave well before pushing me to the 'muthal kettu', the reception area. My house was typical of the [1]agraharam which constituted three parts; 'Muthal kettu' (the receiving quarters), 'Irandaam kettu' (the living quarters) and the 'Moonaam kettu' (the utility), and other sections of the house. The centre of the house was characterised by a courtyard with a sunken floor and an open roof recently secured with a mesh grill for safety reasons.

I saw the boy while walking towards the guests to serve coffee and *bhajji*. To my amazement, the look of him changed my mind. He was tall, well-built and sporting a small moustache. His lips wore a permanent smile. However, I wanted to talk to him and had been looking for a chance. I got the opening after serving coffee and snacks. The boy's father asked his son whether he would like to talk to me privately. Before the boy could answer,

---

1   https://en.wikipedia.org› wiki › Agraharam
INTERNATIONAL JOURNAL OF ENGINEERING SCIENCES & RESEARCH TECHNOLOGY SUSTAINABLE QUOTIENT OF TRADITIONAL HOUSES – A PANORAMIC VIEW OF AGRAHARAMS IN AYANAVARAM Ms. J. Safrin, Rex Dulcie & Mr. C. Ezhil Maran.

I said I would like to. The boy just looked at me with quizzical brows and shrugged his shoulders in agreement.

When we were by ourselves, I asked the boy whether he liked me. "Yes," was his reply in one word and he smiled showing his neatly packed teeth. He did not ask me whether I liked him, which I felt was odd, and reserved it as a reason for a fight later. I mentioned that my concern was about my further studies and I wanted an upfront answer. "Can I pursue higher studies after marriage," I asked him bluntly.

"Is it a pre-condition?" he asked jokingly.

"No. It is a desire I wish to express at the outset so that I don't have to appeal later," I clarified.

"Well. I welcome it but hope you would not mind carrying out your studies in Chennai." He implied by the statement that I can't stay back in the village after marriage. I liked such an undiluted expression which showed inner strength.

"Yes, if it does not upset the routine in the family," I doubted.

"My parents too, would welcome it. Is there anything else on the wish list?" he asked me with his charming smile.

"Do you have any condition for me to abide by?" I enquired in return, looking straight into his eyes.

"Yes," he said, which gave me a slight shock. I nearly laughed when he said I should see that my parents fix an early date for the marriage.

My mother and maternal aunts had lectured me for two days on how I should behave during 'pon parkal'. They were worried about my open request to converse with the boy. My mother and maternal sisters who had almost concluded that the function had flopped were delighted to hear that we had agreed to get married.

"What petition did you give to the boy?" My aunt was always apprehensive of me.

"I just said that we will have kids only after my studies are complete," I joked and got a nice pinch on the waist.

"What demand did he make?" Aunt cooed behind me.

"Nothing except that he wanted me to tell my father to fix an early date for the marriage." I said and ran away crossing the courtyard to the large backyard. My mother and aunts were surprised to see the shyness in me and laughed. They made a comment which I could hear in the backyard. 'God'! The calm boy must have been lured by her fair skin and long raven-black hair. They pitied the boy. He had failed to see the tigress in me.

My father was surprised at the desire of the boy to conduct the marriage in the village in the traditional way. The boy had seen me somewhere in the month of October and the marriage date was fixed in the middle of November. The family had to make all the arrangements in a very short time. But in a village that was not a problem at all. The village took me as their daughter and everyone worked to complete the chores. There was no auditorium in the village; hence, a 'Pandal' was drawn close to the Durga temple at the far end of the broad road that divided the lined houses. Ladies took care of preparing different snacks; a must in a marriage.

Family members flocked from nearby villages and rushed with me to a town in the adjacent state famous for silk sarees etc.. I had no choice. It was all decided by the elders as required during different stages of marriage. I said nothing while purchasing ornaments since I had no affinity for sarees, gold or diamonds. When I look back over the years I lived, I do not remember wearing them on any occasion. They remained in the bank locker. However, we were treated with respect since our family was known for our wealth and influence. Friends or relatives never dared to ask me why I never bothered to dress or adorn myself with the two hundred-odd sovereigns given for dangling on my neck, ears, nose, wrist, hip and ankles. I remember the scene before the day of our marriage when the 'odyanam' I was supposed to wear was found missing. My grandmother appeared on the scene and hushed up the talks and simply went to the locker in her room and fished out her 'odyanam' which was looking as good as new as a replacement. Our family guessed who had stolen it. But knowing the plight of that family, everybody was asked to keep quiet by my grandmother.

Guests who had come in two buses from Chennai were all accommodated in different houses in the village. Except for 'pattanapravesom' and 'nalungu', the rest were performed as prescribed in the Vedic rites. The boy seemed to genuinely enjoy everything.

Our first night was arranged in one of the rooms on the first floor of my house. Father had made it plush with all modern items. I drove away my friends who followed me to the bedroom. Before I came to the room I saw Radhika, my dear friend whispering something secretly into my husband's ears and both burst into laughter on seeing me. Before I could catch her she took flight out of the room.

Narayana and I just sipped the milk brought by me in a jug. While sipping the milk I inquired what my naughty friend had told him about my temperament.

"Oh. She just said I should be careful with my words and deeds. Otherwise, I was sure to get a kick in the shin similar to the one suffered by your pet dog."

"I was then a kid," I laughed.

"Lucky that you were a kid otherwise the doggie would have kicked the bucket," Narayana laughed. "Your friend hinted about your other exploits also," he said casually.

Radhika, you deserve something, I marked it mentally.

"I heard you got some nice beating from Father after your swimming expedition." He continued to tease me.

"Oh, that monkey has told you about that too," I clucked.

Of course, my days after Father moved to our village had been quite joyful. I was known for my notoriety and mischievous expeditions and the villagers have hyped them into stories. Our village was on the northern bank of the river Bharatha and I regularly went to the river in the evening for a bath with friends. The river was about 100m wide in that particular section. I was a good swimmer and ventured from bank to bank on most days. Once on a late evening during one of my expeditions, I swam to the opposite bank betting with my friends despite the warning of the friends that the river was getting swollen minute by minute. Probably, they had opened the dam. That's the bet, I said. Before it worsens, I will be back. But I could not swim back due to the unusual gushing of water by the time I was to return to our bank. The sudden rush of water was not unusual in that season. But such a volume of water in such a short time was unexpected and I got stranded on the other bank. Seeing me climbing the banks on the other side, my friends ran back to the village and alerted my parents. By the time my father managed to organize a search team to cross the river, the locals on the other bank escorted me back to our village through another route. Of course, I was punished.

There was another incident when I got spanked. I took off the golden chain around my neck and put it around the neck of a cow in the village, which ran away with the chain and it was lost forever. Though my father was known for his sanguine temperament, I was the only member in the family who dared to challenge the military man, I boasted to my husband.

We laughed heartily exchanging jokes about our youth.

I was good in studies. I went to the only college in town after completing my schooling. I got married just after the formation of the State of Kerala at the age of nineteen. It was not an early marriage when compared to that of my mother who got married at the age of nine and Father was then only eleven. My maternal aunts used to joke that when it was time for 'mangal sutra' father and mother played hide and seek and were dragged to sit in front of the holy fire for tying the nuptial knot. Theirs had been a long-lasting friendship since then and I understood how they respected and loved each other.

I completed my post-graduation and then went to London for my Doctoral studies. Meanwhile, a son was born to us. After my return, I joined as a lecturer at Madras Presidency College.

My son was born when I had just completed my post-graduation. He was a healthy, charming boy. He seemed familiar with this life. He used to have his timely milk and coo for some time and sleep at prescribed hours. But made sure his mother was near him always.

My grandmother who lived to her 90s told me, "Ambulu (my nickname), you are lucky to have a quiet child. Otherwise the kid would have suffered your tantrums." Of course, I had a sanguine temperament like my father. But grandmother had not lately lived with me to experience how calm I had become in the last couple of years. Since the boy was calm, I had time to read and interact with my friends, so my irritability had no opportunity to burst forth. I was offered a fellowship to pursue a Ph. D.at Southampton University in London. My husband and parents-in-law were happy and suggested that the child who had shifted to solid food and bottle could be left with them. I almost thought of forsaking the offer because I was unsure whether I could manage without the child's and my husband's nearness. My husband assured me that he would follow me shortly with the child on some business proposition. Since there was no direct flight from Chennai to London in those days, I boarded the Air India flight via Amsterdam from Bombay to reach London. I somehow pushed through the first six months in Southampton suffering the pangs of loneliness and several times thought of returning to my child and husband. However, I was Alamelu the terrible, as my mother puts it, and I braced myself to complete the goal. I got busy with my studies.

My husband, as promised, landed in London with the child with plans for starting some business in Southampton. That was a venture not in tune with his business line. However, he risked leaving India entrusting his business to one of his cousins. He had no fear with his father at the helm to oversee the whole business. He spoke with his business friends in London and finally decided to open a small restaurant in West End in Southampton. His friends helped him to obtain all the necessary licenses. A restaurant was inaugurated within two months of his arrival christened 'Kamakshi'. Since Southampton was already a favourite location of many Indians, he did not find it difficult to get cooks to prepare various Indian cuisines. We shifted to a double room flat.

Once my husband was near me with the child I remembered 'God' for some time. I was not an atheist but believed that God created us for a purpose and there was no way to escape the rigours of life. Whether you pray or not, life will sail you to different shores and you must voluntarily or involuntarily endeavour to get acclimated to the vicissitudes. We just formed a kind of robot-like way to respond to external stimuli, interpreting the same and acting in a way conducive to our vibes. I was pleased with myself because *I remembered God when I was happy and not at the time of distress.*

There were two temples in my village. I seldom visited them, unlike my friends who were regular in the evening after the constitutional bath and merriment for the 'Deeparadanai' in either one of the temples. My mother used to chide me for abstaining from accompanying my friends. But my father held the opinion that feeling must come from within and not out of extraneous compulsion. My grandmother who ceased going outside the house ever since my school days told me that if God was omnipresent, he should also be present in you and within the four walls of the house; hence, there was no necessity to search for him outside. I took that excuse to be belligerent.

The restaurant slowly picked up. My husband had named the restaurant in remembrance of his great-grandmother who had toiled in the kitchen of the palace of the Cochin Royal family preparing a variety of food like 'muruku', 'cheedai', 'boli' and several sweets for them. By the time we left London the restaurant had been shifted to a better building and one of his friends was given the charge of running it. They shared the profits, about which I never bothered to ask him. My son was four years old when I secured my Ph. D. and all of us returned to the shores of our beloved country.

My son was growing well. I found him to be over-sensitive to things happening around him. Though apparently, he did not seem to respond to them, his calmness was a worry for me. I used to discuss this with my husband who would ignore me, commenting that I read a lot of crap in psychology, which was the problem with me. "You are like a boy scout who learned to tie knots and tied knots in everything he saw. When the Boy Scout was asked to milk the cow he tied knots in the ……," he would tease me.

Narayana

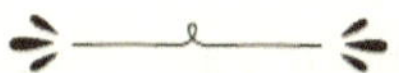

We were a family that migrated to Chennai from Kerala during my grandfather's days. It was a kind of reverse migration during the antiquity of relocation of Brahmins from Tamil Nadu to Kerala. The known past could be connected to the great exodus in the 14th century of the Brahmins to Kerala in batches; one branch trekked from Trichy to Palakkad and another marched via Madurai, Ambasamudram to Thiruvananthapuram. The part of the group who reached Palakkad moved further to the southern Princely states of Kerala looking for a job and safety.

To dwell upon their ethnicity, Brahmins were a population group who shared a common cultural background or descent. They had migrated from Iran, mingled with the great Dravidian culture and settled in North India for a time and then travelled again in batches to different parts of the country. Our story can be very well connected and interrelated to the mass departure of Iyer families from Tanjore to Palakkad, especially during the medieval period, which is documented in migration history. Again, the reasons behind such migration were under dispute. It seemed to have been triggered either by the Muslim invasion that commenced after the death of Pandyan ruler Maravarman in 1310 A. D. or due to repeated drought in the Kaveri delta during the period.

Another reason could be the invitation extended to the Brahmins of Tanjore by the ruler of Palakkad offering land and privileges in retaliation to the boycott of Namboothiris. Our family had been one among those who joined the bandwagon.

[2]History shows that the first wave of Iyers settled in Palakkad district at the beginning of the medieval period. Our family belonged to the Vadama sub-sect which meant those from the North and my forefathers from the paternal and maternal sides wore 'gopi chandana' with a red line in the middle as against the 'Vibhuthi' of other Iyers which indicated our Vaishnavite leniency. It is recorded that the Vaishnavite settlers in Thirunillai and Pallippuram villages were the last group of Brahmins to land in Palakkad from Tanjore or Trichy. Our Vaishnavite forefathers would have been part of the Vaishnavite settlers in Palakkad. My wife's forefathers, who were also Vaishnavites, seemed to have settled in Thirunillai, a village known for Vaishnavite settlers. My father's family was one among the lot who migrated from Palakkad to Cochin and Travancore regions; a migration that commenced in the 16th and 17th centuries AD. Grandfather had narrated to me the agony they went through while relocating to Guruvayoor and from there to Cochin State walking miles in the hot sun.

The marching of our family ended when they settled in the precincts of Poornathrayeswara, a Vishnu temple, probably around the 19th century. Grandfather used to dramatically depict their arduous journey, showing how they endured bruised feet, carried children, bore ancient vessels on their backs covered in tattered clothes as their muscles strained and their bodies became increasingly soaked in sweat along the rugged path.

However, I did not see any tinge of emotion but for distinct detachment while narrating the saga of woes. This untiring ability

---

2   https://en.wikipedia.org › wiki › Iyer

to march long distances must have come with the migratory instincts ingrained in the genetic makeup of Brahmins.

My father had also been trekking many kilometres on school days. The asset possessed by great grandfather was his knowledge of Sanskrit which was acknowledged by the royal family of Cochin, who appointed him as teacher in the lone school in the area. It was a great boon to the family and great-grandmother found a job in the palace's kitchen. His younger days were not that relaxing in the atmosphere of a joint family which was mired with contradictions.

Grandfather completed his schooling in the adjacent village. He was quite a brain, sporting a desire at heart to study law. His father did not know how he could afford to send him to a law school. But one of the royal family members asked grandfather to complete the degree course and then approach him. His father managed a seat for him in a college in the town and found lodging for him in a dilapidated house in the backyard of a hotel run by a friend. He shared a room with an intelligent boy who later went on to join the Central Government Service. Grandfather stayed there for three years with meagre facilities. The friends shared a single table and bench, burning the only hurricane lamp in the night for studies. They both found sufficient light under the street lamp when kerosene was out of stock. They had a routine and when they entered the nearby hotel, they did not have to place any order because three idlis and coffee would be placed by default in front of them as they could not afford a penny more than that.

In the afternoon and evening, they shared one meal. There was no coffee or tea in the middle of the night to invigorate him. He used to slip his legs in a bucket of water drawn from the nearby well to keep awake at night. Despite such constraints, he came out brilliantly and the royal head who promised his higher education gave a letter of introduction to the law school Principal in the town directing him to waive the study fee for the entire course.

Grandfather's happiness knew no bounds. Father used to say that Grandfather never appreciated noisy talks and liked short sentences on any subject. He liked no adulteration in the conversations and did not entertain any exaggerated versions of incidents. He did not have many friends. He completed his course with flying colours and enrolled in the bar. Since Grandfather started his career under the British, he emulated many such characteristics and demeanour. My father had always felt him to be a 'Karma yogi' immersed in Karma without any strings attached to it.

In a couple of years, he became a magistrate. He was known for his well-balanced judgements and everybody appreciated his vocabulary. No one can expect a boy from a remote village to master a foreign language so well. It was when my father was in middle school that the great axe fell on my grandfather's career devastating the family. Grandfather, one day, suddenly resigned from the post and came home all dejected. My father could not understand the reason. Mother was not shocked but cried profusely. So, she must have gotten wind of it earlier. My father did not dare to ask him anything. One day when my father was back from school he saw his mother and father packing the belongings at home. Naturally, he thought they were preparing to shift to a new house since they were to vacate the magistrate quarters belonging to the Government. There were some rumours in the air about his resignation. Since the media was not so brutally popular in those days, the news did not have far-reaching access. Many people visited him and persuaded him to change his decision because it was not his fault. The Judge passed judgements relying on the material evidence on hand and he had made no mistake. It was okay if he did not want to occupy the judge's post. But he could continue to be a member of the bar and so could practice; Father had heard one big shot suggesting to him. Even the royal family member who had sponsored his law studies came to him and had an 'in camera' discussion.

However, the said member was all praises for him and left appreciating his decision. Grandfather's father, the Sanskrit Sir, who was alive, then patted his son's shoulders approving his action. "The brave never allow their minds to dip in depression. Brace yourself and find another way to make a living," his father stated, leaving him to think. They would not be in this position now if Grandfather had allowed despair to win over his heart. It was not about money and the possessions the family had, but the peace of mind with which they lived. I remembered the words of my great-grandfather quoted by my grandfather every time. 'It is not our desire to live but the very act of living is regarded as an obligation and opportunity to fulfil the aims of creation and participate in God's eternal drama. Tradition holds, my grandson, that dharma (righteousness) is the Purushartha (primary aim) of human life since it is the foundation upon which one develops the wisdom and creation to pursue artha (meaning) and Kama (happiness) without compromising the chances of 'moksha' (liberation). Our family is so entrenched in bhakti (devotion) that it is difficult for anyone to deter our will'.

Later, when his uncle came to his school to get a Transfer Certificate, my father understood about their proposal to shift to a faraway place. That night my father was called by my grandfather and placing him on his lap, told him they would shift to Chennai.

Father was not worried about the shift. But seeing the vacant eye of his father he sobbed embracing him. Grandfather told him that he had pronounced a wrong judgement in one of the cases and that his action was a self-inflicted punishment for the same. Father being a child at that time could not understand him. But when he came of age he couldn't help appreciating his sincerity towards his job. Grandfather had in fact gone to the victim's house to compensate. But that proud mother of the victim had spurned the offer and sent him back. 'Had she accepted my little help', grandfather said he would have regretted more since that was a cheap way of atonement.

The mother of the victim had sent him out to seek expiation renouncing something dear to him he deduced and decided to resign from the job which had been dearest to him. The post gave one power to decide the fate of others. 'And see the most supreme one had passed another judgement condemning me as a misfit for the job. I accept His judgement whole heartedly', grandfather had mumbled into my father's ears.

Grandfather and family boarded a train from Willingdon Island to Chennai and went to West Mambalam to the house of one of the distant family members who was an advocate in the Chennai High Court. He too persuaded my grandfather to practice in Chennai. Grandfather said he wanted to quit the profession outright and requested that nobody talk further about it. My father got admitted to a local school in Mambalam and my grandfather later decided to work in a small publishing house run by a businessman as one of the editors. The job paid enough to sustain a a three-member family and Grandfather shifted to a rented house nearby. He continued working in the publishing house. By the time I completed my schooling he had become the Chief Editor and the businessman who had expanded his business empire moved to Coimbatore handing over the entire publishing house to my father retaining a 15% share. Everybody thought Grandfather had forgotten the past and was happy. But my grandmother alone knew the sleepless nights that my grandfather spent blabbering things she could not decipher.

Father completed his schooling and preferred to write the National Defence Academy entrance exam and got a high rank. After a year of training, he was sent to the Military academy. He became close to my wife's father during the training time and later they were posted to different places. But they kept in touch with each other.

After fourteen years of service, he resigned from the post and joined as a senior manager in a firm making bearings for all types of vehicles. He later thought of having his own small industrial house and initiated one automotive wheel bearing industry by availing a hefty loan from the Bank. However, he was lucky that the automobile industry picked up momentum in the early 80s. Business flourished, and in a couple of years before I completed my engineering, he expanded the business further. The publishing house of my grandfather was also doing well with the changed atmosphere in the country. His appearance in business houses became rare and he got fully entrenched in writing his mind. A few novels of grandfather appeared in the market and the writer in him heaved forward with a few successful ones.

Once I completed my engineering, my father wanted me to do an MBA and fortunately, I got admission in Boston, USA. My father could afford my yearly expenses until I got a full scholarship. When I returned, he appointed me initially in the sales division and later gave me the charge of running the manufacturing unit. We bought a small iron ore mine in Karnataka and ventured to a beneficiation plant availing all the licenses. It was a tough job for me to organise everything in an unknown field. We marketed beneficiated ore to Iron industries for two years and later envisioned a sponge iron plant. When we were in the process of commissioning the plant I got married to Alamelu.

Alamelu

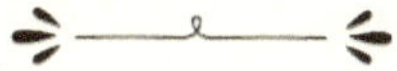

We were living a peaceful life when out of the blue the debacle hit me in the form of arthritis which impaired my activities. It occurred soon after my return from London. Narayana consulted several doctors and confirmed the malady to be rheumatoid arthritis. Doctors suggested steroids as the ultimate cure. Narayana was reluctant to put me on steroid courses and hence took me to Kottakkal Arya Vaidya Sala. I was an in-patient there for three months. Once I was relieved of the excruciating pain and started gentle walking, doctors relieved me to return home, suggesting a strict diet and medicines. My husband stayed back in Kottakkal for the entire three months. My son again happened to be with my parents-in-law when I was admitted to Kottakkal. I had told Keerthi, my son, about my condition and why I had to leave him. Just as before, suppressing all his feelings he had bid goodbye to me.

On return, I was under the care of two nurses. My son used to come near the bed but would never dare touch me or ask anything. His eyes used to be moist and I knew his longing to have a private moment with me since he had a lot to tell me. I used to tell him to sit on the cot and talk. But he wouldn't. Instead would run back to his room. I told my husband to be watchful of Keerthi since I felt him to be feeling lonely. At the expense of his business schedule, Narayana tried to be with Keerthi whenever possible. Despite his insistence, Keerthi would go back to his room during sleep time. I prayed to God for the first time because an unknown fear was clutching my heart with regard to my son. I apologised for not realizing God deeply in my life. I was not worried about my health and impaired mobility. Keerthi was exceptionally good in his studies. But his rustic manners made me nervous.

In six months, my agony had lessened. Joint pain had totally disappeared. My old charismatic upright walking returned, though I had lost several pounds. In a year I regained all my lost strength. One day when I was walking in the garden in front of my house, Keerthi, who had just arrived from school came to my side and held my hand and started crying loudly. I nearly fainted at this unexpected spurt of emotion. That night I could not sleep. Though Keerthi was a calm boy, his violent outburst of emotions did not justify his usual behaviour. Was it that he was suppressing the sensations unnecessarily at this very young age? I had told him several times to come out with what he felt about matters. But he never would and his feelings seldom reached the eye, which was the mirror reflecting one's spirits.

Was it that my knowledge of human psychology was confusing me, as my husband observed? When days passed, my routine started changing. I made it a point to visit the Ganesha temple early in the morning. On weekends I made sure to visit the Anjaneyar temple which was a bit away. My parents-in-law were silently observing the changes in me but never commented. Since Narayana used to be on tour most of the time, in the absence of a driver, my father-in-law drove me to the temples. I used to interact with teachers in the school to learn more about Keerthi. They did not report anything unusual except his history teacher who found an uncommon penchant in him for the subject. He wanted to know more about the characters in the historical times than other matters. He had a few friends but he was digging books in the library most of the time. I made it a point to spend at least an hour with him in the evening during his studies and would lie with him for some time until he slept. I started teaching him slokas and narrating stories from the scriptures. Since I was brought up with my grandfather and grandmother at home, they imbibed in me the bhakti cult and taught me Shastras. As my mind was impervious to the spirit behind scriptures and since I thought those formed a road for escaping the realities, I had not given much attention to them.

However, the unknown fear about my son was of late compelling me to find peace of mind in spiritualism contrary to my convictions. Probably, the seed sowed in me had started germinating. The essence of Shastras was in me, which started germinating in me, prompted by the unknown fear about my son. Was it that God was teaching me a lesson?

Lately, I have been reflecting on my character. Though I learned several things from my grandparents, my interpretations always were quite contrary to the spirit of the teachings and their meaning. However, I was never against the scriptures. But had been saddened about the way the ritual, creed, cult, faith, and dogma had dimmed the beauty of the philosophy and condensed it to the level of mere religious instinct. The influence of various beliefs over the masses had been challenged many a time and many interpretations had been infused compromising the main theme. But I felt the fusions had reshaped the deliverances and seemed to obliterate the main idea. That had led me to shy away from them all these days.

I had a feeling that the beliefs or the philosophy were not that appealing to me any more and many people remain confused about what is right and wrong in their lives. They have never been able to choose the path to realize the essence. They all read superficially or the interlocutor never bothered to read the philosophical connotations along with the stories enunciated in the scriptures. I had heard a discourse on Srimad Bhagavatham. To my amazement, the discourse ended with the death of Krishna without deliberating on final episodes where the kernel philosophy remained. When I asked Sastri about it, he said people never stayed to listen to philosophies.

It was a surprise to see the number of scriptures on our beliefs. We had always considered all arts, sciences, and occupations as sacred and in many ways, the great thinkers of the time had offered opportunities and guidance to perfect one's love for the superior power by way of some scriptural prescription. There were scriptures for meditation, administration, love-making, dancing, grammar, architecture, temple worship, and so on and so forth.

Several discussions had erupted between me and Narayana, whose faith was beyond corruption. Indian scriptures span fourteen fields of knowledge (vidya) and four complements to the Vedas (upavedas), Narayana explained. The fourteen fields are the four Vedas (Rik, Yajur, Sama, Atharva), the six Vedangas (meter, etymology, phonetics, grammar, astrology-astronomy, rituals), and the four Upangas (logic, enquiry, sacred history, code of social conduct). The four complements to the Vedas are medicine, politics-economics, warfare, and fine arts. The Mahabharata, Ramayana, as well as Sankhya, Patañjala, Pashupata and Vaishnava, form part of Dharma Shastras.

Narayana elaborated that over a period of time, the belief system had grown laterally, absorbing more and more ideologies for the refinement of the art of living. However, it seemed that the populace instead of delving into the depth of the message had become more formalistic and ritual driven. Probably, the visionaries in those times thought rituals were a way to put our thoughts under control imposing certain rigidity for tiding over certain situations or to control or dominate the masses.

These formal and ritual-driven external pressures had weaned the individuals away from the core themes and dimmed the prospects of awakening the natural spiritual potentialities of the Self. The mushrooming mediators between God and the individual had further diminished the prospects of the real seekers of true spirit. Recently, we have been in a rush to make a living and in such a hurry many among us never bothered to acquire the correct knowledge from these scriptures. People had embraced the ritualistic parts to appease God heads with a misunderstanding that the ultimate aim of life is to secure pleasure. Those practices had grown to new dimensions, manifesting as a show of authority, money, dominance and other ugly faces. The followers of all religions suffer the same fate, Narayana lamented. "The need of the hour is actually to understand the essence of the scriptures and all the paraphernalia attached to them require refinement to suit the time for the survival of the beliefs." Narayana reminded me of the words of Acharya Sankara about the requirement of such changes in order to keep the core values alive.

Though I was not satisfied with his answers I feigned mollification at that time since my mind was always getting derailed.

Narayana was no fool and understood my pretence. He asked me to think differently before turning to the other side, adjusting the pillow to comfort his head.

"With time the basics have been amended and various additions have been integrated into the scriptures. Subsequently, the need for refinement arises when certain laws become irrational and are deemed unacceptable by society," Narayana murmured before sinking into sleep.

Narayana had told me on several occasions when we broached the subject, "Alamelu, just look at the history of our traditions. You can see that the scriptures were exploited by certain sections fanatically sticking to out-dated forms, meaningless routines and unjustifiable social stratification, which were derogatory to the dignity of the human individual. But looking at the system of caste merely from the perspective of allocating functions to individuals and groups according to their capability and knowledge was something reasonable and we could not avoid such differentiation since people are born with different abilities.

Acharya Sankara says in Brahma Sutra Bhashya that without identifying with the body as Brahmin, Kshatriya and so on, one cannot perform many of the rituals. So even the Vedic rituals are based on avidya. A hurdle is the feeling of superiority or inferiority based on one's identification as a Brahmin or Sudra. Even the identification with sanyasa ashrama is a great obstacle for a seeker. Hence, shastras say that a real knower of brahman moves without any insignia on their identity – (Vidvan v linga vivarjitah). It is further clarified by Acharya that an enlightened being is an *avyakta lingah avyakta charah* ie. 'He' cannot be recognised through insignia or rituals. He hides himself perfectly like God. Hence, identification with the body is said to be 'Vikalpas', an illusion.

Another problem was the language of the scriptures and that its meaning did not reach the common people. This language barrier had been exploited by a section that never allowed the permeation of scriptural knowledge just to ensure their monopoly. This has happened even during the time of Sri Rama when Vedas were out of reach for certain classes and Sri Krishna also subscribed to the strata system. However, Sree Krishna's aim was social order. Mixed interests will never enable one to excel despite inherited qualities and capabilities, Sri Krishna believed. Not everybody could become scientists, warriors, or good businessmen unless they had the mental abilities, which was a trait and such special groups were a requirement in the society to make it impregnable. It was felt that Sri Krishna never meant for class division to occur but distinction as per the functions was made.

Though language played a role in class distinction, the mere translation of the scriptures alone did not solve the problem. There should be a willingness to transform the mental attitude which could be brought about by the spirit of education alone. The emphasis of 'Smriti' was on the spirit i.e., the concentration of the intention rather than the letter of the law or the mere mechanical adherence to the formality of the law.

Narayana

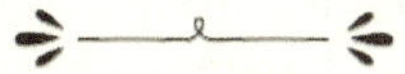

Keerthi was seven years old when my wife, who had strong dislikes towards rituals, doubted whether it was time for his 'Upanayana'. Suppressing my rising surprise at her suggestion, I went to my parents and consulted them. Father immediately phoned Alamelu's father and they chatted for a few minutes. Finally, it was decided to carry out the same in the village where our marriage occurred. In the last seven years, we visited the village only twice. That was when Alamelu was bearing her child and later had to show her child to her grandmother who never wanted to step out of the village. Alamelu's parents also did not have a chance to come to Chennai because of her grandmother.

During the vacation, we fixed the date for 'Upanayanam'. It was really hot in the village but better than the sweltering sun of Chennai. We were just a dozen people from Chennai who attended the function. The rest of the crowd belonged to the village. The villagers who helped us during the time of our marriage were there to ensure the conduct of Upanayanam as prescribed in the scriptures. Not that the villagers had no other recreation but they consider every function in the village as their family function and extended help without asking. Most of the youngsters in the village during our marriage time had left seeking jobs outside the state and several of them had become either residents of Mumbai or Kolkata. A large number had migrated to Bangalore or Chennai and even to foreign countries.

However, the youngsters never failed to congregate in the village during the time of annual temple festivals. They contributed so much that the temples in the village had acquired a new look. I was sorry that I was born and brought up in a town and did not have a village to fall back on to rejoice like this one. Keerthi was unusually happy. He made a surprise request to me to show him the place where my grandparents had lived. I didn't have much knowledge so my father, who was enjoying the company of his friend, geared up to take the boy out to those places, extending his stay in the village. The other relatives left on the third day of the function.

My father was so happy that he borrowed the car of his friend and took Keerthi to the place where his grandfather had originally settled. The place was now difficult to identify with the façade of buildings and shops. In the place of the school building where his great-grandfather taught, stood the Sanskrit college. Father took him to the palace museum just for him to get glimpses of royal times. Keerthi enquired whether he could see the kitchen where the great, great-grandmother toiled. It was a task for my father to convince Keerthi of the difficulty of showing him such private places. Father showed him the line houses where they resided. "Was he walking three kilometers every day?" Keerthi asked, sounding pitiful.

"Not three kilometers dear. It was a six-kilometer walk to and fro," Father clarified.

Keerthi's next sojourn was to the Maharaja's college where grandfather studied, the law college, and at the end of the day, to the place of stay of great-grandfather in Thottekkat house near the college ground.

My father once back home asked me why I had given him so many details about my great-grandfather.

"Keerthi liked hearing these types of stories and when it came to the tale of our family his inquisitiveness was boundless," I said casually to Father who seemed a little restive.

"What made you uneasy?" I queried.

"Nothing, I never had such inquisitiveness as Keerthi, despite the fact that I left for Chennai when I was his age. Probably, I had developed a dislike for Cochin because of the debacle that occurred, which forced total displacement of my father. My father seemed a bit more frazzled as he spoke.

I did not want to prolong the talk since I never wanted to kindle the forgotten memories of those tragic days. So, some un-burnt memories were remaining in him. I too felt I should not have elaborated in such detail the difficult times of my grandfather and those of his parents to Keerthi. Keerthi was too small a boy. I did not imagine that he would take the saga of the family so seriously.

We were planning a return after a week. But Keerthi wanted the entire vacation to be spent in the village. Alamelu was also on vacation and it had been years since she had spent time with her parents so my father said to let her and the child stay back. Since I had many official matters to attend to, I returned to Chennai with my parents.

I was happy to hear from Alamelu, about the exploits of Keerthi, every day over the phone. He was regularly getting tutored on the 'Sandhya vandhana'. He also attended classes on Vedas run by Parasu Vadhyar on the temple premises. Parasu was acclaimed to be an authority in Vedas and his 'ucharana sudhi' (clarity in pronunciation) while reciting manthras was beyond comparison.

Alamelu

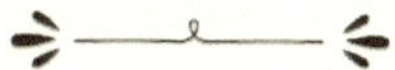

I wondered how much I had missed the calm and serene village atmosphere all these years. Every day I used to take Keerthi to River Bharatha which ran just two hundred metres behind our house. He wanted to learn how to swim and I started teaching him. Of course, my father used to follow me for fear that I might swim to the other bank leaving Keerthi behind. "Old habits never die," he would laugh and say. Keerthi and I were visiting the temple every day. The calmness that I had lost was descending on me.

On some days, Keerthi would sleep with Grandfather in the 'Rezhi' (courtyard) and ask him about his military days. Father appeared ten years younger when he was with Keerthi. My grandmother, shy to enter ninety years of age used to prepare special sweet and savoury dishes for Keerthi, which he consumed appreciating great grandma's expertise. He, who appeared to be a recluse, made friends with children of his age in the village and I was happy to see the reserved boy playing 'dhayam' (an indoor game), 'Kuttiyum – kolum' (an outdoor game), 'marbles', and sometimes cricket etc. with them. Though the village had acquired a facelift with street lights, gas connection, TV etc., the old systems were intact. A group of villagers carried out the procession of a music band along the streets singing bhajans in the early morning, while a few asked for alms, symbolic of 'uncha vrithi'.

Keerthi was amazed to see all of this and wanted to know what they symbolised. Grandfather was having a tough time answering him. Sometimes Parasu, the teacher would explain to him during his 'Veda' class. The villagers gave us a tearful farewell and my grandmother, a rather tough character, kept cuddling Keerthi for a long time. Grandmother finally seemed to be wishing that we leave for Chennai since she indirectly suspected that she would lose the 'vairagya' she had been practising all these years. 'I will become another Bharatha', she feared. She was an inclusive woman and a model for the people who were getting older. "Never bother except in circumstances when you are unable to function on your own. The children are busy with their jobs and the unabated demands of their children and physical ailments creeping in because of tensions from within and outside. Our inquisitive nature and demands would further torture them. Therefore you resign from your desires and confine yourself within," she used to advise her friends who had only complaints about their children.

On the way back, as expected, Keerthi raised the question of who was Bharatha. "I know Mother. It is not Bharatha the legendary King mentioned in Mahabharatha, the epic that grandma mentioned. Then who was she talking about?"

I was wonderstruck to see his newly acquired knowledge from my father. "Grandma did not mention Bharatha, the King, of course. It was about Bharatha Muni who had renounced everything and fallen back into the material world with the entry of a 'deer' to his hut in the last phase of his life. He forgot his austere life and developed an emotional attachment to the deer which caused his birth as a 'deer' in the next life with knowledge of the past. This knowledge made him shun away the world and finally, he attained liberation." I told him the story in the simplest way possible to satisfy his curiosity.

Once back in Chennai, Keerthi appeared serious with his studies and routines. He completed his board examination and as expected came out in flying colours. He joined Chennai IIT electing Computer Science. He was exceptional, his lecturers remarked. However, I did not want him to be exceptional but absolutely an average boy with the ability to understand this world.

He got a scholarship at Stanford and proceeded to pursue higher studies the year my parents passed away. Grandmother who had reached the heavenly abode a few years earlier must have received them all happily. My father's earlier generation were 'janmees' (land owners) and we had a lot of landed property. A big chunk was lost with the introduction of the Land Reforms Act by the State and the remainder of the land on hold was sold by Father considering the maintenance it required. After all, how much land do we need once dead? He was trying to develop detachment. He had become spiritual in the last years of his life and with my mother's death; probably the loneliness had compelled his mind to take a deviation. Narayana and I had persuaded him to come with us to Chennai. He would not. My aunties who were widowed years ago were staying nearby. They found strength in Father and they also stayed back in the village. They too were reluctant to leave the village with their kids. Food was no problem since aunties would prepare and carry a portion to him. He would never fail to attend the spiritual discourses conducted by Sengalipuram Anantha Rama Deekshidhar, Chinmayananda ji and others. I was not sure how far he succeeded in detaching himself from worldly matters. He died after a brief illness. I reached him before the day he left his mortal body. I did not cry but sat holding his hand the whole day.

I stayed back in the village for a month completing the formalities to get the documents necessary for transferring his belongings. I was my father's only legal heir. Keerthi, who had come on my father's day of death, opined that the house may be retained and I agreed to his suggestion and put a caretaker in place.

Keerthi

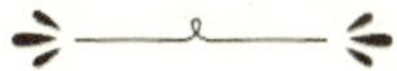

Don't ever think that I scribble a personal autobiography. I am just ruminating about my young days in an attempt to laugh at myself. I know that all the changes apparently seen in me are superficial and I remain as I had been before.

They say time is a predator that stalks us all our life. But as far as I am concerned, the tick of the clock is not actually stalking you; it only reminds you that it will not return. I have missed several of the ticks while passing through school /college days, and sitting on the patio of my apartment at Stanford I wonder whether the road on which I travel will ever end.

I was born into a beautiful world. No doubt. I have wonderful parents. However, I was growing up carrying a little filth in my mind which kept me restless. I would never blame this world for the pleasant or unpleasant happenings in life. 'The bare fact is that we have chosen our own destiny and if the take was bad, how could the world be responsible?' I remembered my mother's words.

See how beautiful it is to look outside the French window of this house. Am I to enjoy the bright sunlight or the skyline dotted with buildings? The trees and plants with sprouting leaves that herald spring are quite a sight after the harsh winter that just receded. The buzzing of bees, chirping of birds and gnawing of squirrels would enchant anybody. The quack of mallards, ducks and swans gliding on the pond's waters amid the apartment complex and their diving at times to catch the prey are sights that would soothe anybody's heart. The world is beautiful indeed and we tamper and make it ugly. Our mind is also likewise beautiful. We manipulate it with unwanted feelings and make a mess of ourselves.

I can't help remembering the narration of the story of '*Pridvi*', the valiant king from Srimad *Bhagavatham* by my mother. 'On seeing the ravaged earth '*Pridvi*', the valiant King took the bow and was about to shoot the arrow to the bowels of the earth when Mother Earth appeared before him and prayed to save her from his wrath. Was it she who caused the devastation? No, it was the avaricious beings on Earth that ruined her wealth. She pleaded politely that nothing was lost or hidden by her. Everything was there in her womb. She was keeping everything deep in her for fear of further destruction. The beings, she said, have only to choose what they want from her. And people started picking according to their liking from honey to poison, reflecting their character. Now, could Mother Earth be blamed for what they possessed?

The simple philosophy is you are what you want to be and don't ever blame this world for what you are. What does this have to do with my life? The answer is that I chose my interests and made myself the person I am now. If at all there were misfortunes, they had all been my creations and I don't dare say the world cheated me.

Many years had gone by. I don't think of yesterday; it shied away quickly, making way for a better tomorrow. Tomorrow had become today, and today would become yesterday. . They say I have become a young man, another form of mine that has survived death—a body transformed into another shape and size.

As far as the world is concerned I have grown tall, intelligent and handsome. But I feel my mental state remains the same. Just as in everybody's lives, many things have occurred in my life too. Good or bad have been etched in my heart for life. A few were disturbing but forgettable, while a few have almost scorched a part of the amygdala, the almond-shaped structure within the brain that integrates emotions, emotional behaviour, and motivation.

What I mostly cherish are those middle school days and before that the sweet kindergarten days. The best incidents in life are often those that were once considered to be the 'Days of shame and failure'. But those days taught me some endearing and funny lessons that moulded my character to a certain degree.

I was around four years old when my mother and father gave me rigorous training for singing a song during the annual day meet in the community while we were in London. I was so excited and had been practising the few lines day in and day out. The dining table and couch in the apartment all formed the podium. My grandparents who had come and joined us for a vacation were enjoying my tantrums. Seeing the zeal and zest of the lad, the parents expected their boy would make a hit. With the day approaching I was too excited and the song taught was buzzing in my brain like a beearound a flower.

The day and time arrived for the performance. I was dressed in a striped shirt tucked in full pants for the evening. The bowler's hat on the head covered most of my small face.

I had never been a brave child and I was all nervous while climbing the podium. But I somehow took a bold brisk walk to the mike as if shaking the fear that had almost paralyzed my thin legs. Raising my head, I pouted the dried lips to commence singing the lines. Then that occurred. I went totally blank. Remembered not a single line of the song rehearsed for days. I kept mumbling something for a few seconds and then the ground ricocheted with my raucous cry and that was the best song I ever sang. Father jumped onto the stage and scooped me off and I remember having sobbed the entire evening on my mother's shoulders. It took years to shake this shame off my memory. I know it never fell off fully, instead slipped deep in and in the heat and pressure of the later events in life, it metamorphosed into a big joke/shame that I enjoyed/endured even now. That was not an isolated incident in my life that got hammered into the recesses. Forgetting became a habit I learned over time, without which I might have ended up in the nuthouse long ago. However, this incident at a young age transformed my attitude toward studies later in school and college. I made it a point to read a matter not more than two times, with no further revisions, and no mugging in study holidays. I wanted to think for myself and create a theory that I had been very successful in my studies.

For me, my father and mother were my world even though my grandparents were living with us and several servants could be seen walking up and down the palatial house in Chennai. Though I was still a baby of fifteen months, I had felt my mother's absence for some time when she went for her studies to London. Since I did not whine much, the family thought the child had gotten used to the new environment. Later, when she fell ill with arthritis and was away in Kottakkal, I again missed her for several months. I had been with my father once to Kottakkal and could not stand the agonies she was going through when the treatment was being carried out. When she was back, I could not recognise the emaciated figure and I did not want to see her in that form. I feared she would die though I did not know what death really meant and that I would miss her forever. I avoided seeing her and failed even to notice her steadily improving health because of my preconceived notions. I realised I had gotten her back when day I saw her walking on the lawn of our garden while coming back from school. She was looking good, shining like an old charm. I clasped her hands, looked at her and cried a lot as I embraced her. Mother was rather shocked at the display of such emotion. But she did not show her feelings except for stroking my back.

I started growing up as a meek boy who feared rain and thunder. A loud sneezing or shade of anger on people's faces would scare me terribly. I was keen to listen to stories. Mother used to feed me with stories from the Puranas, and make me chant slokas and certain Vedic hymns. Father used to tell me about the history of our country, the wars fought by our Kings, many of which in his opinion were unnecessary bloodshed. I was keen to know about our family history. The story of the migration of our forefathers, the rigours they underwent. Neither they nor the later generations have settled anywhere. As far as our family is concerned, Father would narrate that we travelled from north to south and again situations compelled us to move northward. I do not know what you, the generation after me, will do. Of course, I have landed in the US and will get attracted by the different cultures and attitudes of people who behave differently. I have been brought up in a country where people are very emotional and respond to every syllable of other's words. However, I do not see people here who are at least outwardly expressive and sensitive. They may be boiling inside but outwardly not that demonstrative, probably seeking a time and place to exhibit their true emotions.

I have been very much impressed by the saga of my great grandfather whose life and experiences had gotten etched in my heart and I nearly wanted to emulate him. Father used to tell me that the circumstances in which great grandfather's life started and the hurdles he happened to pass through made him what he was. I was to take his words only for a narrative. "You are three generations down the line and in a world which offers you a different atmosphere. You mould yourself accordingly." However, the life of my great-grandfather influenced me a lot.

Transformation again took place in me when I was in the village during my 'Upanayanam' days. My original character opened up unusually. I thoroughly enjoyed the days playing without inhibitions. I seldom had friends in school in Chennai and since we were in a fenced compound I did not know the neighbours and the kids around. The occasional visit to parks and parties exposed me to some kids of my age group. But the duration of such a meeting was limited and hence I was unable to judge a friend. My mother had noted these limited avenues for me to make friends and had taken me to various classes to study violin, swimming etc. But I couldn't make a lasting friendship with anybody. I am not an introvert but a careful bird. However, in the village, during the two months of stay, there wasn't a time I wasn't playing with children. Mother didn't interfere with any of my adventures despite grandmother's complaints and fear of me catching some infection. Mother was enjoying the antics of her son, who had become different. In the evening, I was very busy visiting the temples and hearing stories from the mouths of my great-grandmother and grandfather. The days breezed through and when it was time for my mother and me to travel to Chennai, both were sad. This two-month trip was like a therapeutic treatment given to me.

Once back, I was immersed in my studies and the routine I was used to. The forgotten fear about my mother's bedridden state and the saga of my great-grandfather waved through my mind at times for unknown reasons. I engrossed myself in wasteful thoughts, wondering what I would have done in such adverse circumstances in which my grandfather grew up. He had carried firewood on his shoulders to the kitchen to help his mother even when he was in Law College.

I completed my pre-degree and came out with flying colours. In fact, I wanted to study law. But my teachers, who found a natural talent in me for science and mathematics, suggested studying computer science. Father and mother left me to my decision. Finally, I completed my engineering in computer science and decided to try my luck in Universities in the USA for post-graduation and I got admitted to Stanford.

I did not know what I was doing after I entered Stanford. After six months, I lost interest in computer science but continued my studies rather mechanically. I found a good friend in Samanta, who was doing a master's in Cognitive Science. She was interested in philosophical debates... We used to spend a lot of our time discussing and digging in the library searching for new materials to score points with each other. "Is it a 'love of wisdom' or an activity to understand the fundamental truths about ourselves or the world in which we live?" Samanta would frequently quote the definitions provided by philosophy and laugh.

"Don't we have to get an understanding of what we are and how we are related to this earth and what is the fall out of such a relationship?" I would laugh and join in.

Samanta was from Athens, Greece. But she was related to India through her grandfather who had fallen in love with a Tamil girl from Kumbakonam and married her. He had returned to Athens with her and had got two boys from her and Samanta was the daughter of the second son. "So I am half Indian," she would joke.

"Nobody is a cent percent of any country. You talk about your hundred-year history. Dwelling upon my ethnicity I am the descendent of the migrated lot from Iran who mingled with the great Dravidian culture and settled in north India and then travelled in batches to different parts of the country. That was much before the Indus Valley civilization. The ancient geographical origins of Brahmins – a prominent ethnic group in the Indian subcontinent – have remained controversial for a long time. The results showed that Brahmins had genetic affinities with several foreign populations and also shared their genetic heritage with several domestic non-Brahmin groups. [3]The DNA test data shows the Dravidian language speaking Kerala Brahmins are: 43% South Indian, 39% Baluchistan, 4% Caucasian and 6% NE European, I joshed in return.

"Yes, Keerthi. The population around the world is a mixture and we claim lands and fight on ethnicity," Samantha grinned in disdain.

What arrived first: the chicken or the egg? If God created the universe, then who created God? If nothing existed before the Big Bang, then what created the cataclysm? The laws of the universe dictate that something can't come from nothing or thin air. As a species, we have always struggled to explain how the universe as we know it originated. Religions have always tried to fill this gap in our knowledge, with mixed results. A prime example is the ancient Greek creation and myth, which begins with chaos. Chaos was an incredibly fluid and confusing concept in ancient Greece

---

3   3https://link.springer.com>article.

– sometimes a place, sometimes a goddess, and sometimes quite literally nothing, Samanta lectured.

We started getting close.

Once when Samanta was in financial trouble, I offered help. "I need to save money to send to my mother. I shall accept it as a loan and repay you before you leave the country," Samanta was hesitant to accept the offer.

"Sure, I would never let you leave as a debtor," I had assured her.

Our friendship grew stronger and we dared to talk to each other about our personal lives.

"My first love experience was a failure, Keerthi," she said when we tasted our dinner in a restaurant. I did not respond to her but wondered why she should talk about this to me. "I loved an American and started dating him. He was intelligent and loving. I started living with him on the condition that there would be no physical contact until I decided to marry him. He agreed. After three months of closer observation, I found several disgusting habits in him and left him leaving a note. I do not have any regrets," she said.

I heard her patiently. But did not ask her what those disgusting habits were. "Well, Samanta. A student of Cognitive Science should not have failed in her observation," I wanted to lighten the seriousness.

"Then I was doing a degree in Clemson and went clumsy," she joked without mirth.

"We will stay just as intellectual friends," I said with no conviction. Samanta agreed with doubt hanging in her eyes too.

I too had given her details about my younger days, my mother's illness when I feared she would die, though I did not know what death was at that age.

"You said she was doing well now and why should you think about the past? You seem to hold that fear still," she stated casually.

"I don't know. Those scenes play in my dream every now and then," I expressed my desperation.

"I don't have to tell you that death comes for everybody. Once dead, what is left, is the fragrant remembrance," she was a bit serious in her observations, which I did not like.

"You know, Keerthi, my father died when I was eight. He entered a drunken brawl with his friends and was killed on the street. I did not cry but heaved a sigh of relief when the police came home to inform me. It is not that I hated him. I loved him, but looking at his mental agony, I thought it was better for him to die than suffer. I was too young to solve the problems then. My mother was upset for a few days because she lost her companion. Though my mother called him useless, he had been useful as a protector for us. She kept working in a store. Fortunately, I do not have any siblings to worry about. The church where I went for choir helped with my studies but when I aspired for higher studies the church expressed their inability. I was unsure all these days whether to return to Athens after my studies or bring my mother here. Now the problem seems to be solved because my mother has found a companion in one Security guard. I am going to be alone either here or there," Samanta poured her saga without any emotions.

I wanted to be like her, bold enough to open up my heart. But as she put it, my emotions squeezed out like paste from the tube depending on the pressure. She said my only dramatic presentation was on my great-grandfather and his spurning away of the post and migration to a new place.

"Your great grandpa had done what was right for him and he never complained. Why then are you emotional about it on the account of the exodus of your forefathers from north to south or south to north," she chided me. "Take it as a cinema scene. We do feel with the characters shown on the screen. Once out of the theatre, it is a mere story to be shelved in the back of your head as an experience," she lectured. I did not show her the reactions it generated in me. But she was no fool. Later, I refrained from broaching this subject with her, even when she continued to pour out the day-to-day happenings of her life. "You have to drain them all out with a filter to strain only the soothing ones." Samanta's nonstop advice has become an irritation recently.

For the next few months, we were both busy with studies but made it a point to meet every weekend for coffee or dinner, which would last for hours because of our arguments on different subjects.

Sometimes she used to sit cool without interacting as if in a dream. She would only comment once she was jolted back to the world. "Don't you think, Keerthi, that the logic of dreams is superior to the one we exercise while awake," quoting Etel Adnan.

"Of course, I agree, Samanta. We spend a third of our lives in the unconscious reaches of the night. We try to realise our dreams when we are conscious and when we are awake we still dream without knowing the destination."

"We originate the dreams, Keerthi, and we are astonished to find ourselves in there as dreamers and the dreamed," Samanta would brood.

I avoided talking about dreams since I was always disturbed by weird dreams, and the minute I did not have anything to do, my thoughts would acquire wings and take off to unknown frontiers. Probably, Samanta knew about my weaknesses and sometimes I felt her reading my thoughts.

I felt Samanta was gently evading my company. I thought she had a wavering mind and so could never form a long-lasting friendship. I would be leaving for my country in a few months, so I did not bother about it. She has given me some wonderful days and I should be grateful to her. We especially enjoyed the trips to France, Greece and Italy during the summer break.

We discussed and planned a break. Our first stopover was in France. We visited medieval cities and the Alpine villages in France. Samanta was not interested in Paris, famed for its fashion houses. She wanted to have a look at the classical art museums including the Louvre. She was just happy to see the Eiffel Tower from a distance. The Louvre stopped my heart with its historical art collection. The sculptures, objects d'art, paintings, drawings, and archaeological finds took my breath away. We had only two days on our schedule and we walked throughout the day, exhausting ourselves, and the days ended with hitting the bed on an empty stomach.

We were discussing our French experience during the three hour train journey to Switzerland. Samanta wanted to know why I was so glum in medieval cities and so happy while visiting villages.

"I was just thinking of their likely miserable life in the forts and I was so impressed about the simple living of the villagers and the sincere reception given to us. But I was truthful, I didn't like the 'chevre' (the cheese made out of goat milk) though they call it a special luxury."

"For a vegetarian like you everything is smelly," Samanta complained. "I thought you had gone to the times of your predecessors' long walk and your penchant for village life is abnormal to a city boy," she teased me in a lighter vein.

I ignored the first part and agreed that I liked the village life for no reason. I gave her the details of the days I spent with my mother in the village during a vacation. I went on detailing my visit to Finland with my parents some years back. I will not forget the days in Mikkeli south of Joensuu in NE Finland. A friend of my father took us to those places. I tasted Rye bread for the first time in that village and started liking it very much. More than the bread I liked the simplicity of the villagers. We travelled far to Rovaniemi and Tankavaara in Lapland. It's known for its vast subarctic wilderness, ski resorts and natural phenomena including the midnight sun and the Aurora Borealis, the Northern Lights. From Lapland, we dashed through the tunnel to Skibotn in Norway. We boarded a train from Rovaniemi to St. Petersburg, from where we flew back to Chennai. Did I get a little talkative? I restrained myself from talking further on the trip.

Samanta understood the excitement I had witnessed on the trip to Finland. "What did you do in Tankavaara?" she would not let me stop.

"We were taken on an excursion to places where people used to pan soil to win gold. They used to conduct competitions."

"Wow. Were you lucky to pan out gold?" Samanta genuinely asked me.

"No. That pan was too heavy for my hand and the water was too cold." I answered seriously.

It was a short train trip and we reached Zurich in the afternoon. We immediately geared up to glance at the well-preserved old town filled with medieval and Renaissance buildings and the next day made quick visits to art museums. We had not planned to visit Switzerland but squeezed it into our journey to Italy.

While we were in the Vatican, Samanta wanted to just roam around the Vatican. She said having been born a Roman Catholic she should at least see the home of the superhead and Roman sculptures. We took a quick look at the famed 'Laocoon' and His sons, Raphael's Rooms and the Sistine Chapel famous for Michelangelo's Ceiling.

We were running short of time. Samanta had promised her mother to visit home after a gap of five years and so we decided to fly from Rome to Athens. We reached her mother's place early morning. She had told me we were also meeting her mother's new boyfriend. 'Probably their marriage will get solemnised during one of the days we are there', she had speculated and so planned a four-day stay in Athens, the longest in the trip.

Samanta

My mother was staying in Egaleo which could be reached by metro train from the airport. I was happy to meet her despite the tortures I suffered at her hands. All my cousins had left Athens a long time back for good and there was no contact. Moreover, Mother had estranged her parents and relatives by marrying Father. So, I have only one relation left on this earth and that is Mother.

Keerthi remained in one corner of the couch in the hall witnessing the melodrama of mother and daughter hugging and crying on one another's shoulders. Agnika, my mother showed Keerthi the place where he could dump his things and sleep. It was a single bedroom apartment with one restroom. I was a little embarrassed for the fear of making Keerthi uncomfortable. I had forewarned him about the discomforts he would encounter at my mother's place. It was not the place where we lived before I left Athens. My mother had sold the house father had made toiling all alone. It took him over two years to build it. I remembered having helped him carry planks and other materials when the roof was paved. His friends had also assisted him in the difficult jobs. How the same friends caused his death was a matter that intrigued me even now. It was an independent house with two bedrooms and two restrooms and a large attic where guests could be accommodated. Mother had sold the house, the reasons only known to her after I left Athens. She must have fetched a good price for the house and I had no idea what she did with the money.

I did not want her to lie and cook up a story so I did not ask her. She had pocketed my father's gratuity from the company he worked for too. When I asked her whether she could part with a portion to fund my studies, she had complained about settling the liabilities her husband had left her with. I got fed up with her lies, which was one reason I decided to find my own resources. The method used was considered abominable from the perspective of the society I lived in. Though society never helped anybody in difficult times, it had an opinion on anything you did. That was the best help one could expect from society. I did not blame them since the people around us were all mired with problems and so in order to escape their miseries they would fan the woes of others seeking a relative solace.

It was a rented apartment where she lived now and I had no idea how she managed to make both ends meet. The job in the restaurant was not that remunerative. I had told Keerthi that if he wanted, I could book a room in the nearby hotel. But he opted to stay with the family rather than lying blinking at the roof in a hotel room. He remained on the couch nursing the mug of tea I brewed for him while mother and I kept engaged, exchanging news which we could not communicate over phone or letter in the last five years. At times Mother cast a sly look at Keerthi and muttered something to his embarrassment. Mother suspected him to be my lover and warned that I might face the same tragedy she endured. I told her that of course he was my boyfriend and even if I decided to live with him it was none of her business. Our heated exchanges were literally in Greek that Keerthi could not have followed, I hoped. He was not the inquisitive type and hence I did not worry.

We spent that day at home and the next day we moved around the city, which was named after the Goddess of wisdom and warfare 'Athena'.

Athens was the largest and most influential of the Greek city-states. It had many fine buildings. Keerthi liked Athens and Athenians for their invention of democracy. He had wondered several times about the condition of people around the world if democratic Governments were not formed. He recalled the collection of essays of E M Foster, 'Two cheers for democracy', and was talkative on the same.

I relished the company of Keerthi for two reasons. 1. He was a good man and 2. His unique character served as study material for me. I have met and been close with many boys in my five years of living in the USA. They were either introverts or extroverts or they acted to be either one or the other. But I had not encountered one so balanced and deep as Keerthi. From the days of our acquaintance, I suspected that he wasn't what he appeared to be. Something was bothering him. Probably, a thorn stuck in his mind from a very young age. He had not been able to pluck it out while he was growing. I wanted to study him better and help him. And if I was wrong then God should have the great heart to excuse me since I was using him as a guinea pig for my experiments without his knowledge. I regretted it internally but continued my studies.

I had been truthful to him on several matters. My early life had been miserable. My parents were not that poor but had no extra money to spend. In fact, my father earned well, being a good mechanic and he had a permanent job in a nearby factory. But he spent 70% of what he earned on drinks. He never thrashed Mother or me when he reached home inebriated, which was a regular scene in my neighbourhood. Once back home, he would get to one corner of the bedroom and snore his head off. In the morning he would promise me and Mother that he would come out of his problems one day and be good. On some days he would come with presents and flowers for me and Mother, filling the house with groceries, cakes, milk etc. But that became very rare with the passing of years. He had a complex about his looks. He was dark, probably taking the gene of his mother. His friends were not kind to him, teasing him at work. He was tall, well-built and handsome, and my mother had accepted his love and married him. However, she too became critical of his dark skin later; probably after my birth and commented that she had been wrong in marrying him, challenging her parents' objection. Most of the women in the neighbourhood were homemakers and they spent their leisure time gossiping, and one of their topics of gossip was my father's complexion.

My mother's love and marriage were in a way an escape from the poverty of her parent's home where she lived with several of her siblings. Though poor, her parents were not short of ego about their heredity and lineage. Her parents as well the relatives had deserted her for marrying my father. She boldly encountered them until my birth. I was more Greek in appearance than a south Indian and so father was happy that I didn't have to suffer the insults like him. I think over the years Mother too started slighting him, which he could not bear and he started finding solace in drinks. It was accentuated by his friends who relentlessly teased him with nicknames and finally, it ended in a street brawl and his killing. Once he was dead, Mother understood the pinch for money. She had a tough time thwarting the hawks flying around in the absence of the protector. She was not very educated and so could not get a decent job. We managed somehow. I was then just eight years old and was getting free education in a school run by the parish in the locality. Luckily I had a sweet voice and penchant for music. The church I visited for choir took pity on me and offered to take care of my studies. I wanted to study and get out of the house. So with grit, I learned my lessons and did exceptionally well in high school. I did not know how I could pursue further studies since the church expressed its inability to support me further. I was aware that with my limited educational qualification I would not be able to fetch remunerative jobs. My ambition was much bigger, so I just wanted to make money and leave the country. I knew that my mother who was working in a restaurant would not be able to promise anything and in fact, she was nagging me to find a job to sustain myself.

"How long do you think I could support you? You are grown and it is high time that you stand on your feet," she taunted. I never had any affection for her right from a young age because she was cruel to my father. I had a liking for Dad but hated his complex and drinking. Mother had married him not out of love but to escape poverty, she had said to me. I expected her to repeat similar gimmicks to evade the current situation for she was not ethical enough. Luckily, she did not opt to run away with somebody immediately after my father's death and leaving me in the lurch or maybe she could not find a suitable prey. Thank God that I was not left to languish under the care of a stepfather. I was thankful to her that she protected me from the jackals prowling around the house. Therefore, I was indebted to her for the shelter provided until the time I left Greece. I felt that it was my duty to help Mother secure a safe life for the help she had offered me till the day I left Athens. I knew this could be my last meeting with her and that we were departing in two different directions thereafter. With this in mind, I helped her by borrowing a lot of money from Keerthi so that she could undergo certain cosmetic surgeries that would make her look younger and more attractive to her new lover.

When she informed me about the company she had found in a widowed security staff, I was relieved that I did not have to carry her burden. In this context, I remembered the story Keerthi had told me about a 'rishi' who was left with some sages at a very young age by his mother, who was doing odd jobs in their kitchen. The boy, a born intellect, wanted to run away, forsaking everything. But his mother was a burden and a great hurdle for pursuing his search for enlightenment. One day his mother died due to a serpent bite. The feeling he had then was a great relief instead of grief since she was an obstacle in his quest for acquiring 'Knowledge' of Brahman. I could not be compared to such great visionaries. My vision was my future and if you call it selfishness, you may be right. But as far as I was concerned, it was just a longing to live quietly without burdening any soul. I did not dream of a royal life or wish to travel around the globe. Then why did I agree to travel with Keerthi? After the days spent with Keerthi, my concepts were gently changing. "You may do what you want and satisfy yourself without hurting anyone or nature," Keerthi philosophised. "Once your mind is quiet and satisfied with the wanting, you are ripe enough to enter an ascetic life." Though I could not comprehend the entire meaning, it struck a chord of unknown longing in me. I assumed I was reading Keerthi but in actuality, Keerthi was exposing the 'I' in me and teaching who I was.

I applied for a degree after school at Clemson University, South Carolina, USA and secured my admission and scholarship. There was no scope to raise money from anywhere for my travel and other expenses. The only asset we possessed was the house we lived in and I did not dare ask my mother to pledge it since I was not sure when I could repay the loan. I was left to find my own resources. I made friends with a rich guy who frequented the church. He had his eyes all over me every time we met and tried at every opportunity to misbehave with me. He was my bait I decided, for realising my dreams. I bluntly told him that it would not be a free ride. He agreed, and on learning of my background, he thought I would be cheap prey. I succumbed to his desire and he tried to dispose of me by thrusting some sheaf of drachma.

I accepted it and told him about my desire for higher education and my plan to fly to the USA. I demanded help with an Air ticket to the USA and some additional money to manage my stay until the scholarship money reached my hands. As expected, he bawled at me and nearly kicked me out of the room. I simply left him. The next day, I followed him to the shopping place that he and his wife frequented and in his presence, I exchanged a few pleasantries with his wife Rachel, whom I had known for a while. I had done several errands for her. She liked my singing ability, my tall stature and golden hair. I had grown into a beautiful lady I knew looking at my reflection and it was obvious that it was the only and best asset I possessed. Rachel used to ask me about how I maintained my sparkling skin. Before bidding goodbye, I said to Rachel that I had a secret to divulge to her, casting a sly look at her husband. He understood my intent and that took the breath out of him. His wife, the daughter of a rich man, was a devil incarnate and her brother was a police officer. He feared her because it was her money he was frittering. It was common gossip in their area that he had married her only for money. Otherwise, for his looks, many girls would have fallen for him. If news about our relationship leaked he would be in a soup and so he came forward to purchase my silence. He asked me to get a passport and then come to him. I used the money thrust into me earlier to complete the formalities for travel. Then fear clutched my heart whether he would help me further. Suppose he did give the money, such a wad of money in my hand would raise suspicion in my mother and a leak of the same might invite trouble from around. There was a possibility that I could be charged with theft and arrested. He had money and none of my explanations would stand against him.

I did not want to back out from my dream of leaving for Clemson and my aspiration made me think for hours to find a safe way to approach him. Finally, I planned to meet him when he came with his wife for her regular hair appointment at a luxury mall. I met them at the entrance and reminded her about our last meeting in the church and about a promise made by a gentleman to help me with my further studies. "Yeah, you did not tell me who that blighter was," she demanded to know and I politely said it was her husband.

"Oh. I never expected this punk to do such great things. I thought he was interested only in the girls' bodies."

He looked at me a little astonished and lost the colour on his face.

"Is it true, Neitche, you promised to help this beauty," she glowed at him.

"Yes, Rachel, I took pity on the girl when she said she had no money to realise her only dream. In fact, I wanted to consult you before I gave her money," he trailed.

"Oh. Neitche," she exclaimed, "I never thought you had such a kind heart. I believed this young girl would become a singer. Well, people have diverse interests. " "Samanta," she turned her attention to me and said, "No worries, dear. Since my husband promised, how could I stand against it?" She flashed a visiting card at me and asked me to visit their office in town the next day.

"Don't you think, honey, we should arrange her travel? Let her come with all the papers. Don't you agree?" Rachel asked her husband in a sweet tone, which generated a creepy feeling in me. I was sure that it had given a jab of fear to her husband as well. Before I could thank her, she started walking into the mall, holding her husband's hand passionately. I saw him falter for a moment before regaining his composure.

It was a sleepless night for me. I wondered what I was in for. I knew Rachel was not a beauty but had brains. I was blocked at the entrance of their office by the security who wanted to know the purpose of the visit. He neither approved of my faded dress nor the shoes I wore. However, my figure forbade him from throwing me out. I flashed Rache's business card in front of his eyes and that did the trick. I waited close to an hour in the front office and then I was shoved in. Rachel was in a different mood. She was the boss here. She did not wait for pleasantries but demanded that I show her all the papers I had in hand with regard to my admission. She made sure that I had not lied. She called her manager and asked him to calculate the expenses I would likely incur until the scholarship was granted. She asked him to prepare a promissory note pronto and explained to me the legal implications of such a note and asked me to sign if I needed the money. I never expected such a turn of events and for a minute I was taken aback. But I braced myself and decided to face the consequences. Rachel glared at my face for some time and smiled when I said that I was ready to sign. I was to clear the entire debt within five years or else legal proceedings would be initiated to recover the money, she warned. She advised me to save something from the scholarship money and do some work side by side to repay the debt. "Your mother is our security, though she is not a party to this," she said mirthlessly. "Then considering your safety, I think it is better you collect your ticket and money as traveller's cheques from this office just on the date of travel. You can sign when you are ready and get the proceeds. I shall keep the promissory note and the copy. I hope you have some balance from the money my husband donated to you so you don't have to trade your body another time," she said very casually without raising her head from the paper she was reading. I was drenched in shame and cursed myself for a second. I did not reply, and when no answer was forthcoming, she lifted her head and looked at me. I saw her wet eyes.

"I don't blame you, child. You have your vision about life. Had I been beautiful like you, I would have done the same to win this world. After all, what is the use of this body other than for realising our dreams? I lack the beauty, the great possession of a woman. But I have money to compensate for it and woo the handsome men of the town to my side. My husband was my employee and I had my eye on him. I bought him by rudely exploiting one of his little crimes. I am happy with him but he finds happiness elsewhere. Let my help be retribution for the sin he committed," Rachel choked.

I simply murmured, "Sorry," which carried the intended message. She dropped her head down and disposed of me with a wave of her hand.

I did not feel guilty for twisting her husband's arm because he had lured many girls of my age for a paltry sum and threatened those who demanded more 'drachma'. Those girls had no dream like me and they came cheap for him. They feared Rachel's brother, a brute police officer. But I utilised his fear of his wife to bleed him. But I had failed miserably in front of Rachel who was aware of her husband's weakness. Was she helping me as retribution for the sin her husband had committed? But was I not a party to it?

What was my punishment? Or what was I to do for atonement? I climbed down the steps of Rachel's office with a heavy heart.

Mother wondered how I managed the resources to go abroad. She did not believe me when I said Rachel was financing me. Rachel appeared to be a treacherous woman to her, and she wondered how she would part funds without any security. I told her about the promissory note and she was wise not to question me further, fearing she would be hooked into it. "That is your problem. Don't ever drag me into it," she said avoiding the subject.

"I happened to toil to settle the liabilities of your father and now you are….." I did not allow her to finish. "You were the liability for my father. He would have been alive had you supported him instead of lashing him with your harsh tongue. Had he been alive he would not have left me begging for money like this," I cried my head out, which stopped her from speaking further. "This house is in my name and I am at liberty to pledge it for my expenses, so don't compel me to do it." That nailed her box. "Now shut your mouth and behave until I leave this place." My retort was a big shock to her. She immediately retreated to the kitchen. I regretted snapping at her. I transferred the title of the house to her name, which settled her misgivings. I wanted nothing but independence from her. I did not know what lay in front of me in the country I had dreamt about.

I knew I had disgraced myself by adopting a tricky way to accomplish my wishes. I did not give much value to chastity and all that stuff. But the purpose for which I had lost myself was repulsive. The guilt in the back of my mind for having sold my body as a commodity for realising my dream continued to hurt me. A poor girl like me had no other asset to pledge, I muttered to myself.

Four years had passed. Still, the guilt in me was aching. I wanted to confide this in somebody and empty my heart. I found Keerthi to be the ideal bin to dump the dirt. One evening, when we were indulging in the topic of virtuous ladies in history, I casually asked him whether he believed in the chastity of women. Keerthi's response was like a jet of water that doused the fire in my consciousness. He talked about body and soul at length and finally said, "You do not have to worry about this body, which perishes with time. But never soil your soul with outrageous acts which will hurt you and others. The body is like clothing for the soul. When the body gets too soiled, the soul changes its covering, throwing away the old one, much like the process of Ecdysis."

I could appreciate the first part of Keerthi's observation that the body was to perish over time. But his statement that "never soil your soul with outrageous acts" was something that pricked my already injured consciousness. Yet having poured out the pent-up emotions, I felt relieved. I had just sold the rotting body and not my soul, which was still pure and pristine because I had not traded it, I tried to console myself. I attempted to read more between the lines to get reassured. It was just a matter of a few hours for mutual benefit. But I had hurt Rachel's feelings. Rachel was also not innocent. She had lured him with her riches and exploited his crimes without seeing her profile in the mirror. He wanted her money and had cheated her with his charms. At the same time, he was maintaining a private life. So, we were all cheats and in turn, were cheated. It was a circle.

I told Keerthi how I managed to land in the USA. Keerthi said – 'instead of living with burning desires and rotting your mind you found a solution'. You did not snatch anybody's property but fixed a price for the trade. Based on what you have shared with me, Rachel was aware of her husband's private exploits and she did nothing to prevent it. She could have tried to release herself from him had it been that unbearable. In this context, Keerthi told me about a rather unrelated but contextual story of his great-grandfather who threw away the covetable post as reparation for the fault he committed. Grandfather's pronouncement of judgment in the court was based on the evidence at hand. As long as the onus of responsibility rested with the accused to prove his innocence, such an inadvertent mistake was common because lawmen always tried to prove their stand and never bothered about the accused. Grandfather had guts to take responsibility and he recompensed by punishing himself. Rachel had several means to end her misery. Her atonement for Neitche's fault would never negate his accountability.

Did Keerthi mean that I should recompense my guilt?, I wondered. Whatever be that he intended I felt relieved by way of tipping my feelings.

.

I did not know whether I had fallen in love with a person like Keerthi, who was a perfect gentleman in my eyes. But of course, my reading of him was that he was not what he appeared to be. He was so soft in his mind that he was impacted by the sorrow of others. One should feel but should not transform oneself into that character, was my conviction.

He had not given a hint of his love for me. He continued to be a good friend and took care of me in all respects. I had not basked in such affection in my life. He saw to every one of my needs. He either suggested ways or helped me physically, mentally or monetarily to rally around the problems. I have never opened up my heart to anyone in the same way as I did in front of him. I never used to mutter or complain because I didn't have a friend or family member to confide in. However, after forming a close friendship with him, I frequented him with complaints, like small kids do. He would listen to me and sometimes with love, he would admonish me. I liked him chiding me and for that reason alone I used to bring in some contentious issues just to enjoy his response and expressions.

He was systematic, decent and had never uttered a lie to me. I assessed him to be spiritual. He was regular in his religious practices and when I mentioned Brahmanism, religion etc. he would say that he did not want to attach his activities to religion, caste, sect, etc.

"I am part of a group of people who followed a specific way of life that isn't categorized as a religious practice. This group of people intend to acquire 'knowledge'. It is not for securing material objects, but as a means to broaden their intellectual horizons to comprehend the 'Brahman', a metaphysical concept that refers to the single binding unity behind diversity in all that exists in the universe. Original Brahmins never visualised any god," he whispered as if in a trance. "It is not a religion, Samanta, but a socio-political ideology within the variable religious dimension. Brahmanism had no missionaries in the religious sense," he would go on explaining for a few minutes. "The practices had been dormant for several decades and the recreated Brahmanism as we see today was not a haphazard collection of isolated features, but rather responded to a homogenous vision of the world. Some opine that Brahmanism is a vision of the world in which Brahmins play a central role. Better let it be described as a vision of Brahmins that has consequences for the world." His discussions resembled Aristotle's inquiries into the nature of existence and understanding the world.

"Samanta, I do not talk about Brahmanism as it is known today. Brahmanism, according to some of the [4]scholars who have researched its rise and fall think that it initially belonged to a geographically limited area, and may have originally been centred in the middle and western parts of north India. It was in this region that Brahmanism continued with the culture of a largely hereditary class of priests. The Brahmins derived their livelihood and special position in society from their close association with local rulers. This changed with drastic political change in the North, perhaps beginning with Alexander's invasion, which culminated in the unification of much of the subcontinent under Mauryas and ended with many catastrophic invasions after the collapse of the empire. Alexander came from a different cultural world. He tolerated Brahmins but butchered those who stood in his way. Mauryas had no particular interest in Brahmins. Brahmins were under threat of extinction or reinventing themselves. Brahmins chose the latter option. The transformation for survival and flourishing under changed circumstances altered the inherent qualities of Brahmanism.

American scholar, Sheldon Pollock, coined the term 'Sanskrit cosmopolis' to designate this phenomenon of the dominance of Brahmanism and Sanskrit in political inscriptions in important literature on Buddhism and Jainism. The Spread of Brahmanism cannot be seen as a matter of religious conversion. According to some scholars, it is not a religion but a socio-political ideology within a variable religious dimension. Rulers adopted it, did not cover it necessarily from one religion to another, and Brahmanism had no missionaries in the religious sense. Keerthie made a small

---

4   https://brill.com>view>title.

    How the Brahmins won-from Alexander to Guptas – Johannes Bronkhorst-2016

speech and never wanted anybody to call him a Brahmin in the religious sense.

I had stayed in Keerthi's apartment and had seen him meditating early in the morning, muttering something during the day. It was interesting to hear about the function carried out for initiating him into Vedic studies and in order to quench my thirst, he had explained to me the sanctity of the function. I found it difficult to understand him initially. The umpteen number of debates in the last few months had given me some idea about the philosophies he lectured on.

We discussed the emergence of gods in the Hindu pantheon, and I found similarities to Greek gods. There are several gods upon whom we meditate as the immortal or bodiless Brahman. Keerthi used to chant the invocatory verse of Isha Upanishad.

"Om Puurnnam-Adah Puurnnam-Idam Puurnnaat-
Puurnnam-Udacyate |
Puurnnasya Puurnnam-Aadaaya Puurnnam-Eva-Avashissyate" ||
Om Shaantih Shaantih Shaantih ||

However, they are all one among the Brahman, he would conclude. [5]"These deities, which are its foremost forms, one should meditate upon and worship, but then deny (reject the gods' individuality). Thus we unite with the Universe and attain union with the Self.

"Yes. Keerthi. Our people were also agriculturalists who, using animism, assigned a spirit to every aspect of nature. Eventually, these vague spirits assumed human forms and entered the local mythology as gods. When tribes from the north of the Balkan

---

5   Maitri Upanishad 4.5–4.6.

Peninsula invaded, they brought with them a new pantheon of gods based on conquest, force, prowess in battle, and violent heroism. Other older gods of the agricultural world fused with those of the more powerful invaders or else faded into insignificance."

Keerthi had some knowledge of Socratic philosophers in ancient Greece like Socrates, Plato, Aristotle, and the Peripatetic school of philosophy. I supplemented him with what I learned and interpreted. He heard them with awe.

Many times we have had healthy conversations about complex philosophical thoughts and the mind. Keerthi used to say, "As such, the mind is not an organ but a consciousness in the entire body and the mind is only a conduit for the thoughts to pass through. It is 'buddhi' which analyses the thoughts and it is 'chitha' that takes the decisions. Hence, one should keep the 'chitha' clean to stay sane."

Keerthi had secured an internship in a renowned company in the USA, which might win him an automatic position in that company after his studies. When I congratulated him, he in return threw a surprise on me that he wished to return to India after securing the degree.

"Haven't you understood what I represent and the processes in my mind that guarantee my capabilities and my capacity to implement them etc.," he was jokingly elaborating on the goal of the cognitive science I learned.

I did not laugh at his joke but said, 'Better that you know yourself' wishing he acknowledged his love for me.

He laughed at me asking whether I quoted Delphic Oracles' words to Alexander before he commenced his expedition – a clever evasion from the subject matter.

He was either disinclined to tell me that he loved me or he did not love me at all. On the other hand, I was hesitant to open my heart and be the first to reveal myself. I was carrying guilt inside. Was it my grandma's genes from Kumbakonam working against me, making me think along the lines of chastity and all that bull shit?

Suddenly, I wished to settle my debt with Keerthi at the earliest and forget about him, as if it was the debt that bound me to him. I regretted that I was not in a position to immediately settle the loan I had taken from him. He said he would leave his address in Chennai so that I could transfer the amount at any time. "I do not want my girl to be a debtor," he said with seriousness. 'My girl', that expression sent a chill into my heart. I was reluctant to recognise myself. I channelled my thoughts to find a reason to hate him. As I was working part-time with a scientific group for minimum hours that would not attract the wage laws in the country, I wished to settle the debt fast. I was engaged in Cognitive science to replicate intelligence in AI. I was sure of a good placement after securing the degree and the first struggle would be to settle his debt. I swore at my mother who whined for money to beautify herself.

Narayana

I thought Keerthi might settle in the USA. After the meeting with the Greek girl whom we met during our last visit to him in winter, we wished he found company in her. In fact, Alamelu liked Samanta and decided to wholly accept her as our daughter-in-law provided Keerthi entertained such a wish. She found Samanta to be intelligent and loving. She never concealed the surroundings from which she was coming and said she had no relation whatsoever to call when in Greece. Keerthi had failed our expectations and had returned to Chennai with the intention of starting an IT firm designing robots. I did not fully understand his ideas but agreed to help him obtain all the licences from the Government and they offered a space in the Industrial park of the Government. It took four months for him to complete all the formalities and he recruited a few guys not looking at their academic performances but their practical knowledge. Days rolled by. It was summer and Alamelu had gone with my parents to our summer cottage in Kodaikanal. It was a vacation, so she had gone with a bundle of books to while away time. One day I had a call from Kodaikanal that my mother was ill and I rushed there with Keerthi in our car. We started early in the morning and Keerthi was driving. Due to the depression in the Bay of Bengal, there had been heavy rains for the last two days and the mountain road was slushy with mud. While he was negotiating a curve, we saw a boulder roll onto the road from the slope blocking half the road. It must have happened a few hours back because there was no warning sign or people around. Keerthi saw the boulder and applied the brakes but due to the mud wrap on the tires the car skidded and hit the boulder. He was driving at a very slow speed so the crash was not serious. However, the collision propelled Keerthi forward and his head hit the glass and my head hit the dashboard and stunned me. Keerthi, who recovered, saw blood all over my face and thought something terrible had happened to me and fainted. When I regained consciousness, I was in the ambulance and realised that they had given me first aid. The injury was not that serious except for the size of the band-aid. I looked for my son who was sitting near me, dazed. In an hour we were taken to the nearby primary health centre where the doctor declared both of us to be well and permitted us to travel to Kodaikanal. We drove in a taxi from there, arranging for a mechanic to attend to the dent on the bumper and grille and bring it to the address I provided.

I did not know why Keerthi was silent during the trip and I could not cheer him up. I had phoned Alamelu from a local booth so they were not in shock when we reached home. I told my wife to take care of the boy who was still glum. During dinner, Alamelu jokingly said, "Keerthi thought for a minute that you were dead and he has not recovered from the shock." She did not allow me to talk to him further because Keerthi was trying to concentrate on his work to escape the shock. "He has a very weak heart Narayana and I am scared about that. His imagination runs ahead without reasoning and I don't like the signs," she muttered. My mother had a mild attack and she was in the ICU. Since my father insisted on staying back in the hospital room allotted in advance for shifting mother the next day, we both returned home. In a week mother was discharged and Keerthi left for Chennai. Keerthi was back to normalcy but was reluctant to say anything about the accident. He told his mother that he would be back in a couple of days and I could rest until then.

Samanta

True to my anticipation, I got a good placement in a company working on computer simulation, robotics etc. I was excited about the job and I started seeing money for splurging. I saved enough in the next six months to repay Keerthi and I contacted Keerthi over the phone to confirm his account number. Keerthi called me once a week to inquire about my well-being; his mother had talked to me twice during this period. Keerthi said I need not rush to transfer the money since he was coming to the US with regard to his project. On the one hand I was happy to meet him but on the other hand, I did not want to stretch it beyond the point of friendship. I met Keerthi's parents when they came to the US for vacation a year ago. They were decent like Keerthi in their manners. I did not know any other word to describe them and what other meaning the word 'decent' carried was also not known to me. They appeared sophisticated when introduced and while talking I learned that they were well educated. Keerthi's mother had a doctorate in psychology from London and his dad had an MBA from Boston. They were quite unassuming without a taint of pretension and quite genuine. I liked his mother, who was very observant of everything and I felt she weighed every sentence that came out of my mouth though she appeared extremely casual. I searched for a glint of ego in them for they were rich, well-cultured, educated and had seen a lot of the world. But I could see nothing. That was amazing indeed. I have met many people in my country and in the last five years the USA has offered opportunities for me to meet several people from different walks of life. Ego did not allow them to reveal what they really were despite the knowledge that ego hurts our personal feelings more than it inflicts injuries on others. I had thoroughly failed to overcome my ego.

Keerthi's mother on hearing that I had no relations left in Athens replied, "We are all a single-man army fighting physical or mental wars." I smiled in response to her remark, musing that Keerthi took his lessons mostly from her. Could she read my mind? I wondered when she, in turn, said, Keerthi, unlike her, possessed a weak heart. Though I initially found the remark to be out of the blue and odd, later it struck me why she had mentioned it.

We were alone in the apartment. Keerthi and his father had gone to buy dinner outside. "Keerthi loves you Samanta?" her casual, blunt question surprised me. I mentioned that I had no clue, and when asked about my decision, I couldn't provide a straightforward response. She did not wait for me to give her an explanation; she gently patted my hand and said, "You are the navigator of your ship and a moment's delay or hesitation can take you away from the destination. This holds true for Keerthi also," she added. She was right. I had hesitated to confess my love to Keerthi, possibly due to the guilt in my heart or because of my ego, which wanted him to express his love first. Now, he has returned to his country while I remained in the USA expecting him to pine for me and come running. But I never thought of running to him. I endured the thought that I had to settle the debt to Keerthi at the earliest and square the obligation. After this, I could probably start again with a clean slate. I knew this cheap ego of mine was the stumbling block between Keerthi and me. Several boys wanted to date me. I did not feel like dating anybody. I have been teased by guys who thought I was a lesbian. No. I have to try and find somebody who will debate with me on various matters and take my self-esteem to new heights.

I remembered the conversation I had with Keerthi's mother. Sometimes, to get around a problem, our mind may create strange new ideas, no matter how bad or unacceptable they are to us. For scientists, such flights on the wings of imagination enabled them to create models. This was how the human mind made sense. But I was creating models to cheat myself. I had read about the ancient Greek experiment 'The Ship of Theseus' and leafed through Nietzsche's 'Eternal Return and into what be favourable'. In Ancient Greece the concept of eternal return was most prominently associated with Stoicism. Nietzsche claimed the exemplary human being must craft his/her own identity through self-realization and do so without relying on anything transcending that life—such as God or a soul.

When I talked about stoicism, Keerthi's mother mildly elaborated on it. "Yes, dear Samanta. That school imparted virtue which was based on knowledge. They considered that the wise lived in harmony with the divine reason that governs nature and were indifferent to the vicissitudes of fortune, pleasure and pain. I did not believe in such an approach and attitude of identifying with fate and providence. However, I admit that my perception has changed recently due to several incidents," Keerthi's mother jested. We could not continue our conversation because Keerthi and his father had arrived with food.

Keerthi

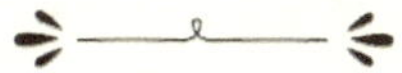

The vacillation of the mind is the biggest dilemma in our life. It is more than the fear of death. I have been brooding and ranting to myself for the last six months about what I really want to do. Of course, I was busy with my projects. Yet, I know I was isolating myself and wondered whether this type of self-inflicted isolation may predispose me to solipsism syndrome. I really wanted to put an end to all this and that was the prime purpose of my visit to Samanta in the US. But I failed miserably. Had the suspense been broken with that trip, my mind would definitely have come to rest. I landed in the US and went straight to Silicon Valley regarding my business proposals and that was also a form of procrastination due to some fear within me, to meet her and express my love. From Silicon Valley, bracing myself with courage, I managed to reach Stanford and went straight to her new apartment. I reached her late in the evening. When I saw her, she came and embraced me, planted a kiss on my cheek and waited for my response. I gently relieved her since the butterflies in my stomach had started fluttering. I could not express anything and sought an escape into the restroom for a bath. She seemed a bit disappointed but masking her feelings inquired about dinner. I suggested a simple dinner at home. She was not a great cook but prepared some grains, potatoes, rice, and pasta and bread was available in plenty. I helped her with all the preparations while talking. I saw the bottles of wine and brandy on her shelf but did not comment.

I couldn't help but wonder if those were her companions when she was alone. I stayed with her for two days and roamed the University campus. Met some old friends and returned to India. She was in tears when I left her and I, too, choked for words but failed to express what I wanted. I almost concluded that she didn't share the same emotions I had for her.

Once back in Chennai, my desperation scaled to new heights and I almost started isolating myself. I was always rapt in thoughts, which reached nowhere. I had slipped into similar moods when young and in those days my mother would engage me in different conversations. "Remember, Keerthi, nothing is too high to get over and nothing is too low to get under. We have solutions for everything in us. We should know what we are and what we want." I wondered whether she knew about the problem I was grappling with.

"I have seen, mother used to tell me that most people hide behind something to forget the problem. Some find solace in alcohol, a few others become workaholics and many tail behind religion or some kind of belief. Some dream about a supernatural entity that is supposed to witness our innermost fears and desires, and they think 'He' watches our soul and our innermost secret selves. And we expect 'Him' to help us overcome loneliness. Sometimes I wondered whether individuals who passionately pursue their interests, such as artists and musicians, might also be seeking an escape through their creative endeavours to overcome feelings of mental isolation. I consider such persons to be weaklings, who are unable to recognise their own feelings and come out of the shell and dare to face the situation," Mother had continued lecturing. Was it an indirect hint of my failure to acknowledge my inner feelings and bravely expose them?

"Of course, my dear son, we have devised methods for cultivating self-knowledge and quelling our anxieties, such as meditation and psychotherapy. However, these practices strike me as forms of self-brainwashing. When we meditate or see a therapist, we are not solving the problem. We are merely training ourselves to ignore or live with it or learning to suppress the horror and despair it triggers. We have succeeded in enhancing the quality of our life, they claim." She went on quoting scriptures and I wondered whether she was advising me yet again to look at my inner self and find the causeative factor for my disturbances.

I remained in thought for a week and finally decided that I could no longer deceive myself and live in disappointment betraying myself. Yes. I know someone who wanted to break free from their inner constraints and jump over the barrier of hesitation to admit the truth living within.

I slept that night without dreams; with renewed energy, I planned to call Samanta and tell her the truth. It must be dead of the night in the US and should I wake up Samanta? I thought it better to wait until our evening when she would have yawned out of bed. I was not aware of my temptation to procrastinate and I again missed the opportunity.

I was in the office early in the morning, blankly sitting in front of the computer waiting for the sun to rise in Stanford to make a call to Samanta. It was at that time Father phoned me to inform me that he was reaching my place in a few minutes and we were to go to Kodaikanal immediately. I was confused because he was supposed to be in Kodaikanal where the family had gone to escape the sweltering summer days in Chennai. "Come downstairs near the coffee place. I have no parking space anywhere nearby. Come down," he repeated and disconnected.

I came down in a hurry and walked, rather, ran to the coffee place and slipped……..

Samanta

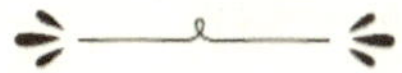

I tried to immerse myself at work and upon returning home, I would inebriate myself to garner the courage needed to confront my fear of failure and the stubborn ego that prevented me from revealing my true self to Keerthi. I became friends with an Irish guy who was working with me. He was also amazed to see the change in me because in the last year or so I had ignored him and he could not understand the reason for my sudden transformation. I told him that if he would refrain from questioning me on my personal matters, we could be friends. He replied that as far as he was concerned, he simply loved me and my past was irrelevant to him.

However, he was particular that from here on the present and future mattered to him and both of us should be true to each other. I heard him and thought about it for a day and I liked the logic behind his words. I agreed. I told myself that I was not deceiving myself. Keerthi had umpteen numbers of chances to express his love and he did not. I was sceptical about his Indian background and the morals he valued. Though apparently, he seemed not to bother about the candid pour of my past deeds and as a matter of fact, approved of the reason behind it. However, his reluctance to openly declare his love worried me. Well, now I have to appreciate his hesitancy and forget about love and all that crap. I need a man for mental and physical support. And I can't live a lonely life. As long as Keerthi was near me, I felt safe and basked in his affection and protection. As far as he was concerned, he must have felt the affection that one has for a sister or a close friend. How long was he to protect me? Over a period of time, one is on their own and one should learn to preserve and protect oneself. My thoughts were going haphazard to justify the decision I was conjuring in my head.

After a week, I told my Irish friend that we would live together for some time and try to know each other beyond the barriers and then solemnise our relationship in the nearby church. I tried to reach Keerthi in his office but could not get him. But I received a call from Ms Alamelu a day later, which changed my future.

Keerthi

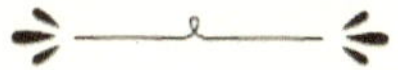

So many things happened in the last two months. Samanta was sitting near me on the dinghy, rowing in the still waters of the Kodai Lake in Kodaikanal. Our marriage was to take place in a week.

Though I had recovered from the fall, the amnesia I suffered had left an unknown vacuum in me. Probably, the events that were to unfold in the future may fill the void and make me absolutely normal. But I am still confused about my parents, though logically, it was beyond doubt that they were my parents. When will I get connected to them and recognise their identity? I kept communicating with them, but the feeling normally expected in a son-mother relationship was yet to develop in me. Samanta has made me promise not to divulge this rather permanent amnesia. I also resolved to give my best acting performance despite the terrible feeling.

I rewound in my mind for the hundredth time the dialogues I had with my parents regarding the events that had taken place after my fall on the pavement.

Father had said that he was sitting in the car when he saw a crowd some hundred metres behind him in the rearview mirror. He got out of the car and walked to the scene, inquisitive to learn the reason for the crowd. He was shocked to see me collapsed on the road. He managed to get me admitted to a nearby hospital. Everything was in a haze for me. When I fully regained consciousness, as advised by the doctors, I was taken to another hospital where they confirmed I had no concussion or so and there was nothing to worry about. But I was sure that I had some problem. *I was not able to recognize my parents.*

Mother arrived by the weekend at the hospital. I remembered her as the figure I had met as an apparition. I nearly swooned seeing the same person. When she started stroking my hair, a chill ran through my body and I could feel the shock waves in her too. She observed my face for a few minutes and shook her head several times. I wondered whether she was not feeling good. She said, "No, dear, I am so happy to be with you."

"It is only a wave of transient amnesia," I heard the doctor saying something like that without knowing how long this transient phase would last. I believed the doctor. She was my mother and the gentleman who was near her was my father. I told myself several times. I wanted something to hold on to in that confused state of mind. I wanted to tell them a lot. Obtaining permission from the doctor, I gently told my mother about my near-death experience. She implored me to recount the events from my accident to my visit to her in astral form, along with her husband. She heard me coolly, embraced me and babbled, "You are reborn to me Keerthi."

Though I could not digest the thought of reincarnation and all that stuff, the sudden relief from something that had been bothering my nights flabbergasted me. Had I been dreaming, as they say? My confusion was confirmed clinically. But the doctor's indication about 'transient amnesia' was really helping me to stay mentally stable. I hoped and prayed that I would get through this state and link myself to reality. Mother, being an academician rather than a clinical psychologist, wanted me to be taken to a practising psychologist to explain my situation.

I was taken to the best psychiatrist and after several sittings, he explained what could have happened to me. The doctor tried to convince me that all the scenes I described to her were manifestations of the fears embedded in me since my very young days.

The scenes with my father and mother kept rolling in front of me as live shows. I kept thinking of the figureless mother, and the words of the figureless grandfather, who was waiting for her to recover from a coma, were ringing in my ears loud and clear. At one point I could connect the scenes. The doctor explained that the sight of my mother in bed was my entrenched fear of her death when she was laid up with rheumatic arthritis. In addition, the earlier car accident had left some anxiety in me. The feeling before I slipped into unconsciousness that my father had died in the accident was still in me. It was filled with my imagination that my mother was dying in Kottakkal and my father was taking me to see her before she died in the hospital.I had fantasized that she had already passed away by the time I arrived, and my interaction with her astral form, suspended in a simulation, had allowed her spirit to re-enter her body and revive her consciousness. It was all a fantasy coupled with the fear ingrained in me that had a dramatic effect. I heard everything and wished the explanation would be true and I never showed my emotions at any point in time.

I thought once back home the familiarities would enable me to remember better. The doctor said after some private talks with my parents that I was all clear to get engaged. While we were driving back to Kodaikanal, Mother gently asked me about Samanta. I was about to call Samanta but….. I regretted having not called her. Father said there was a surprise waiting for me when at Kodaikanal. I could see a kind of relief on the faces of Alamelu and Narayana; probably they never expected me to remember Samanta. I remembered everything but was not able to recollect the faces of my parents.

Samanta was at the door when we alighted from the car in the portico. She came and there took place an emotional drama. I hoped I would recover fully and remember everything with Samanta's coming. Samanta and I both bemoaned the failure in acknowledging our own feelings which could have ended the drama of love much earlier."But nature has its way and we are helpless. I do not talk on fatalism," Samanta remarked and gave a sly look to my mother, who responded with a smile. Samanta dared to ask me one day about my dreams. "No, Samanta. I am not aware of the dreams you are talking about." In fact, the doctor gave me an explanation of the dream I had about seeing a comatose figure in the bed. I have no idea about the other dream and have not understood its meaning. Though I remembered the story of my great-grandfather, I uttered my hopelessness in recalling it. Samanta wanted to resolve the issue that had bothered me for a long time. I had a few sessions with the parapsychologist in the presence of my parents. The doctor, after a discussion with my parents, concluded that it could be the young man who had confronted my great-grandfather in the magistrate court that kept appearing in my dreams.

"Yes, doctor, I remember the story of my great-grandfather" I started excitedly, hoping to regain the lost connections. I was so desperate at my inability to recall the faces of my parents. The doctor just held my hand and explained "Your father had told you about the saga of your great-grandfather a hundred times when you were young and you had got very disturbed about the forced migration of your great-grandfather to Chennai due to the incident in the court. Later, you visited the place of residence of your forefathers and continued to build stories of your own. You had started imagining yourself to be the great-grandfather and wanted to amend the error. At one point in time, you started transforming yourself to be a magistrate and visualised that, that young man was swearing at you. Repeated screening of the events in your mind ultimately confused you. You were unable to distinguish imagination from reality. That caused your dreams."

Samanta clutched my hands, fearing my reaction. I heard everything and remembered the history, but not the dreams which bothered me. I was cleared of those dreams. Probably the injury on my head erased those for good from my memory pad. No stories or reminders of other incidents in life enabled me to recall the images of my parents. I wanted to cry aloud and hammer to my consciousness that Alamelu and Narayana were my parents.

Samanta sorted things out with her Irish friend who was waiting in the US. In the presence of Samanta's mother, our marriage took place in Chennai. The great surprise was the arrival of Rachal to participate in the marriage.

Alamelu

I really did not know my mental state. Anybody could imagine the mental agony of a mother who encountered a situation where she realised that she was not in memories of her son. I could very well distinguish the great act put up by my son to soothe our feelings. But the cessation of the mental bond in him was very apparent. He was really struggling with his inability to put me back on the pedestal I had occupied. I wanted to end the drama we were all playing. I told Narayana, who was also suffering like me, that this could be [6]'dissociative amnesia' due to psychological stress. Keerthi had suffered that. Perfusion of his right medial temporal area which reportedly had decreased soon after the onset of amnesia may be the reason for the delay. There were rare cases where patients recovered after years. Samanta was also aware of it. There was no point in waiting, making his and Samanta's lives miserable so we arranged for Keerthi and Samanta to travel back to the USA. At least that would end Keerthi's mental torture and the embarrassment of Samanta, who was struggling along with us. Samanta used to sob on my shoulders in private, lamenting about providence. She knew the original Keerthi and the tie he had with us. She wished that sometime in the future, he would remember and connect everything. "I will strive hard to do my best to bring him back to his original state," she had sworn several times.

---

6   https: www.ncbi.nih.gov>pmc: Nobuyukimiysui, Yuka oyanagi and Ichrio kusumi

Five years had passed since Keerthi left with Samanta for the USA. He got into the same company where he worked as an intern. He was remotely controlling the company he owned in Chennai.

A series of tragedies occurred in the past five years. Narayana's parents departed for their heavenly abode and, within a year, took their son, probably to relieve him from the mental agony he suffered silently. Of course, Keerthi was near him when he died. Both cried profusely at their misfortunes. Keerthi, still, was unable to remember and Narayana was writhing in mental pain thinking about the same. A few days before breathing his last, Narayana requested everybody to leave the room and wanted me to be alone with him. He died on my lap.

I did not know how to cry since I had been challenging the tears all through my life and the tear gland had lost its functional ability. I resigned myself and never tried to spill a tear forcefully. I just wished to be alone with his memories and wanted to remain so until my day ended. Narayana had not given me any chance in life to aspire for something. He was foresighted. Though I was born with a silver spoon in my mouth, I did not know what to do with wealth since my desires were very limited. I never had any affinity for money, gold or any other material comforts. We both lived a rather austere life and we supported a lot of charity homes, which we never advertised. Our perspectives differed in several areas but our overall goal was to reach the same destination. We never thrust our philosophies on others. Our love had a different dimension. I have a good lot of memories of the pleasant life with Narayana. He did not change a bit right from the day I met him. He had his faith and he never ran away from it in any situation.

I had always challenged the age-old practices in the family, never believed in fate and did not attach importance to spirituality. But he believed that spiritualism was the only straw to hold when sinking in the deep waters of miseries. Whereas, I, the 'incorrigible', as my mother observed, often disagreed with the normal convictions and thought everything was human-made and we should brace to challenge them. But all my philosophies faded away with Keerthi's fall and the days I endured subsequently.

I used to quote [7]the law of wasted efforts whenever somebody failed in their attempt. "Do you know, Narayana, that the lions succeed only in a quarter of their hunting attempts? Despite this small percentage of success, predators don't despair in their pursuit and hunting attempts. The main reason for this is not because of hunger as some might think, but it is the understanding of the 'Law of wasted efforts' that has been instinctively built into animals, a law in which nature is governed. Half of the eggs of fishes are eaten, half of the baby bears die before puberty, and most of the seeds of the plants are eaten by birds. Animals, trees and other forces in nature are more receptive to the law of wasted efforts. Only humans think that the lack of success in a few attempts is a failure. But the truth is that we only fail when we 'stop trying'. Success is to walk over your mistakes and go beyond every stage where efforts are awaited, looking forward to the next stage".

I preached about endeavouring repeatedly and climbing the ladder of success. But had we not been striving all these years to make Keerthi regain his lost memory? Samanta was still struggling and had exhausted all her skills. But Samanta wanted the circuit to be completely connected. Rare were people like Samanta, who had consideration for the feelings of others. She was telling me the other day that she hated Agnika, her mother, but never could leave her alone. She wanted to sever the relationship with Agnika after

---

7   https://timesofindia.indiatimes.co...

she found a life of her own. "But the mother in me did not allow me to disconnect from her forever," Samanta was all emotional. How long were we to continue trying? Narayana never asked me this question. But that question was reverberating in my mind out of frustration, questioning my rationale.

The recent happenings have taken a toll on me. There were misgivings from my side concerning our beliefs. All the teachings at a younger age and the stories told by my grandfather and grandmother were running in front of my mental screen. The narratives of my grandfather were finding new meanings in me though they had only an indirect relation to the cause of misery in which I was. "Alamelu," my grandfather used to tell me, "Those who follow 'Sanatana dharma' are often wrongly accused of advocating fatalism. This accusation stems from the ignorance of the law of the cause, action and effect, otherwise called karma. Unfortunately, we have cultivated a belief in the inevitability of thwarting the misfortunes which the law of karma never meant. You must understand Alamelu that the graphic description of the karmas and their consequences implied in the philosophy and message are for practical understanding. We know we all waver between animal and human instincts. Until we achieve the transformation, we never will be able to come out of this swing," Grandfather used to be eloquent on the subject.

[8]It is like Mark Antony who played with the emotions of the masses after the fall of Caesar, first evoking compassion and then rousing a frenzy of revengeful violence raising the animal passion i.e. the anger in you. The basis of hell and retribution etc. what we see in Puranic Hindu Religion is the deep insight and all-pervading psychology. The seers know that without the stick

---

8   Karmas and Diseases. By Swami Sivananda (September 28, 2001).

you will not be able to control the herd of sheep. They used fear psychology by introducing an inevitable array of consequences if one strayed out of the moral code of conduct and related instances of transgressors who faced punishments. They detailed the results of the sinful actions and how emotional attachments brought grave suffering upon man. It was all for safeguarding society from evil influence and guiding them to the righteous path. Grandfather had philosophised.

So, what have I done to deserve this punishment? If it was not fate or destiny responsible for the unbearable situation and if it was not punishment for the sins I have committed in my present or earlier life, then what?

"Once you know nature and its laws, we will become aware that every action has an effect and that effect is certain to cause some other action and that is how nature balances itself. You can act but cannot stop the effects. Upanishads also talk first about nature and then come to the human aspects, drawing comparisons from nature and asking you to identify yourself with nature. But most of the people chant the Upanishad without knowing its essence but simply enjoy the rhymes and rhythm," Grandfather had bewailed.

If all the happenings in life were for a greater cause, what could be the result of the recent happenings in my life which has drowned me in the pool of miseries and what awaited me in future or what was I destined to endure to balance nature or the cosmos? This was all a confusing endless play. Therefore, I sported simple philosophies which appeared more rational and appealing. But my logic could not help me at the time of distress. As I have not attempted any practical training in spirituality, whenever I cast the anchor of spirituality to moor my ship of thoughts, it mostly slipped the target. You have to keep practising as Sree *Krishna* sermons to Arjuna. 'Put the thoughts in the cage and free your mind which is 'Aananda' (bliss or happiness)'.

Days rolled over to months and another year had passed. I had been in touch with my old friends who were in different parts of the country and they also communicated with me whenever possible. Radhika, my friend, who had secretly told Narayana of my youthful exploits during the time of our marriage, visited me. She had changed a lot and was looking stylish, trim and healthy. With crimson paint on her lips, bobbed hair and pointed heels, she was no longer the village girl I had met a few years back.

Her life had been miserable after marriage. She married someone from a Singaporean family who had settled in Chennai. She had returned several times to her parents in the village, unable to bear the tortures at the hands of her mother-in-law and husband. She had no freedom at home and was treated less than a servant. Servants also have dignity. She wanted a divorce. But her parents never bothered to learn the reason why she was seeking divorce. They believed in forbearance and pacified her and took her back to the husband's place decking her with more ornaments. In fact, I was ready to help her. But she declined my offer and declared that her parents were still living in the 19th century and she would not complain any more to her parents. She would challenge or perish. That was the resolve with which she left me at that time.

I was seeing her altogether in a very different light. When I wondered about it she said, "Ambulu, the death of my father-in-law changed the scene at home. Though my father-in-law always supported me, his voice was getting subdued by the blaring of my mother-in-law. My husband never dared to confront his mother. Father-in-law settled his score with both of them by bequeathing all his possessions in my name. There was nothing his son had earned of his own and so the son and mother were left to my mercy after the old man's death," she chuckled.

Radhika was educated and so she started managing the empire of her father-in-law with his reliable friends who knew the history at home. She registered a complaint in advance with the police that should anything happen to her, the son and the mother-in-law would be squarely responsible. That had tied their tongue and hands. "I never wanted any money or comfort. All I wanted was a child from my husband. But…" she moaned. "His mother fell sick and died weeping on my lap for all the sins she had committed," she laughed. A year back, her husband also passed away. "Now I have decided to live like a queen frittering away all the useless wealth," she guffawed. Was it her destiny or did she walk into this sort of life?

The chain of events right from the death of the father-in-law bequeathing all assets in her name, the later desperations of her husband and mother-in-law, their death had all happened despite her efforts to thwart them from seeking independence. She could not end the relationship and get liberated earlier because of the muddle-headedness of her parents who thought money would solve all the glitches without realising that wealth was the problem in her husband's place. "I am a society lady now and several hyenas prowl around me. Do they want me or my wealth?" She was laughing hysterically. "What is left for me in future, Ambulu? I have no relatives to hang on to. I can adopt a child. But I think relations are not for me and I do not want to get disappointed again. So have decided to fritter away the useless wealth," she sniggered.

Everybody has stories to narrate. She did not ask me anything personal. "Ambulu, I know you better than anybody." With this remark, she left me.

When I was trying to forget everything, completely immersed in the kingdom of Narayana, I received a call from Keerthi informing me that he was arriving with Samanta. Why such an urgent trip?

Is it that, Samanta was expecting? No. That was another ill luck that had befallen the family. It had been diagnosed that Samanta could never bear a child. That means the family line ends with Keerthi. I didn't react to this news and did not expect any miracle to happen.

I did not ask since I had ceased questioning anything happening around me. Keerthi came and embraced me and said he was able to connect everything and now the void in the memories had been filled by recollections of the past. I believed him. So, the perfusion of his right medial temporal area has returned to normal levels after almost seven years, one of the rarest cases. The tear glands in me oddly worked and tears rolled down my cheeks. Narayana was not there to hear him and that thought almost squeezed the breath out of me. I incidentally observed them come with an unusual amount of baggage and they sprang the news on me that they had left the USA for good and had decided to live in Chennai with me. I did not react but smiled. Samanta observing me and my actions bereft of feelings, doubted my sanity and boldly asked me one evening whether I needed counselling. I said to Samanta that my mind was at peace. She and Keerthi understood it.

I remembered the dialogue between Sree Krishna and Uddavar in Uttara Bhagavatam where Krishna enunciated about sanyasam. 'I will strip everything from you and make your mind naked of the desires which will make you a sanyasi.' Was I not stripped of everything? Now was 'HE' testing me by bringing Keerthi back to me? I never cursed 'HIM' at any point for the incidents in my life. I never had such desires for 'HIM' to kill and bare my heart of emotions or attachments except for the maternal love for my son. Am I to stay inert to that feeling also? Now I understand the meaning of the attribute 'Nirguna' of 'HIM'. 'HE is inert', bereft of feeling and wanted everybody to be like him. "Grandmother, if the creations behaved the way in the literal sense of the meaning of 'Nirguna', then how would this world chug?" I remembered to have asked her despite the teaching of the inner meaning. "You are positively negative on every matter." The toothless smile of my grandmother flashed in front of me.

I decided not to give 'HIM' another chance to test me. I left for my village, leaving everything with Keerthi and Samanta. I was happy that Keerthi had suggested retaining the village house when my father died. Was it his premonition?

Keerthi knew I never wanted to recreate attachments like Jadabaratha in the veining period of his life in this world. I remember how great-grandmother avoided touching Keerthi's little fingers when we were at the village on vacation. Great-grandmother feared that the physical contact with his little fingers would make her develop an emotional connection. I remember having told him about the rebirth of Bharatha as a deer. "You are too young to detach yourself," Keerthi had argued. But age is not a precondition for 'Vairagya' to set in. Once I reconnect, I will never be able to return to the detached life, I reassured myself of my decision.

"Mother, I leave things to you. I do not wish to philosophise on these matters. I remember all the teachings you and Father have imparted to me about the mind and the requisite to control it." I remembered all of his mumblings.

Fate struck me again.

I was not living an austere life soaked in spirituality as one would think. I simply continued living alone detached from everything. I was a regular visitor to the public libraries and book stalls and engaged in reading without paying heed to matters which may bring back the memories of the past or create a fear about the future. Keerthi and family were visiting me very frequently.

"If you have tears, prepare to shed them now." I remembered the dialogue of Mark Antony when I regained consciousness in the hospital bed after a severe stroke that paralysed my left side. Why am I not dead? I did not ask the question to myself or others around the bed. Keerthi and Samanta were sitting on the cot opposite mine. Keerthi came near me. His eyes were filled with tears. But recently I have seen that he is reluctant to shed tears. He was getting hardened with time or this seed of mine was gently germinating in him. Since the haemorrhage had affected the left lobe of my brain, my speech was not affected. Yet I was reluctant to converse with anybody. He seldom tried to engage me in conversation except for talking about the details of the physiotherapy drills I was to undergo.

I got the stroke while I was chatting with Keerthi, who had landed with Samanta; a routine monthly visit. Keerthi understood the sudden changes on my face and the guttural sound in place of a rather gentle voice emanating from me. He immediately carried me to the car and drove to the hospital in town at an unbelievable speed in the early morning hours. The haemorrhage was severe and doctors did their best but fate left me partially immobile. I did not respond to any sermons of the doctors. I could visualise the difficult future ahead of me.

Keerthi

Samanta and I shifted to the village to be with Mother who neither entertained nor spurned our nearness. The physiotherapy either in the hospital or in the Kottakkal helped her regain the tone in the muscles. At a point in time, she asked me to discontinue the trials and take her back to the village. She never showed any sign of disappointment. She continued to be like what she was. I used to bring books for her from the libraries and she would sit on the cot holding the book in her right hand and would continue to read until her hand got tired. The dead weight of her left hand was bothering her a lot. When I was off to Chennai to attend to official duties, Samanta was taking care of her. Though my mother rarely conversed with me, she would engage in long conversations on different matters with Samanta. It was difficult for me to understand her feelings despite my knowledge of her character. Probably, she thought that it was yet another test for her. She had the willpower to survive while remaining 'inert' to everything around her. She stayed so until her breath dissolved into nature.

At this point in time, I remember the twenty-four gurus of the [9]Avadhoot Brahmana. However, in my life, I had only three gurus. My parents and my wife taught me great lessons in life and my life itself was another Guru exposing its worthlessness despite the

---

9   chapter 11 Canto 11 of Sreemat Bhagavatham.

power of money and fame. Mother taught me how to stay bereft of everything by emptying my feelings towards the material world. She had everything but she never wished to possess them. She never aspired for anything new and never was perturbed when she started losing things one after another. She believed in getting stripped of all desires before God decided to bare her of earthly materials and taught her to live without them, a lesson she learned from her grandmother.

She considered herself different from her body so the stroke and the partial disability did not bother her much. She used to move in a wheelchair on her own within the sprawling courtyard of the agraharam house. I had seen her just sitting in the centre of the yard where sunlight was harshly seeping through the opening in the grilled ceiling until late evening as though she wanted the resigning sunlight to take her away to oblivion with it. I have not seen her praying to God, except on the occasion when she was recovering from her severe arthritic problems when I was young. She was well versed in the scriptures but she considered them a distraction to cheat our minds and pin our hopes on the future.

My father was different in the sense that he was a devout Brahmin but was not that ritualistic. He never thrust his beliefs on anybody. He had a lot of reservations about religious rituals and spirituality. He never argued with anybody but simply discarded summarily those which did not appeal to him. He believed that the road to that 'ultimate destination' was our mind.

I met a selfless being in Samanta. Though born and brought up in a different culture and under different circumstances, she assimilated into our system and never questioned our practices with many whys and whats. She too did not aspire for a life forgetting her responsibilities. She believed that enjoyment is only a fleeting feeling, but if you could make others happy, that would bring you everlasting joy.

I was a confused person all along but recently I have started seeing not me but the 'I' in the mirror of my consciousness.

"Sum modate modaniiyam hi labdhvaa"
"Having attained the blissful Atman, he becomes happy"

(Kathopanishad Up. I-ii-13)

Glossary

Acharya Sankara – Adi Sankaracharya was an Indian philosopher who consolidated the doctrine of Advaita Vedanta.

Agraharam – A row of houses typically occupied by Brahmins.

Avidhya – Ignorance, misconceptions.

Bhajji – A snack.

Bhashya – Explanatory work.

Durga – One of the goddesses.

Drachma – Former monetary unit of Greece

Deeparadanai – Lighted lamps placed before God.

E M Foster – An English author.

Etel Adnan – A Lebanese-American poet, essayist, and visual artist.

Gopi chandana – Paste of sandalwood marked on the forehead.

Idlis – Rice cake.

Iyer – An ethno-religious community of Tamil-speaking Brahmins.

Kottakkal Arya Vaidya Sala – A century-old charitable institution engaged in the practice and propagation of Ayurveda, the ancient health care system.

Mangal sutra – *Auspicious thread.*

Muruku, cheedai, boli – Typical snacks of South Indian Brahmins.

Manthras – A 'sacred utterance' in Vedism; one of a collection of orally transmitted poetic hymns etc.

Nalungu – A cleansing and purification ritual.

Namboothiris – Malayali Brahmins.

Odyanam – A gold girdle worn around the waist.

Pandal – Marquee.

Pon parkal – Seeing a girl before approving the marriage.

Pattanapravesom – Celebrations related to the entrance of the groom into the village.

Puranas – An ancient and vast genre of Indian literature on a wide range of topics.

Sarees – Traditional dress of the Indian woman.

Slokas – A couplet of Sanskrit verse.

Sastras – Sanskrit word that means "precept, rules, manual, compendium, book or treatise" in a general sense.

Srimad Bhagavatham – A text that is considered one of the main collections of wisdom in Hinduism.

Smriti – That which is remembered.

Sandhya Vadhana – Mandatory religious ritual supposed to be performed daily, traditionally, by Brahmins.

Uttara parva – Kind of epilogue.

Upanayanam – Ritual of initiation that marks the male child's entrance to the life of a student (brahmacharin).

Uncha vrithi – Living by collecting grains by walking the streets in the village.

Vadama – Belonging to northern parts.

Vidvan – A person who has knowledge of a particular science or art.

Vibhuthi – Sacred ash.

Vaishnavite – One who worships God Vishnu.

Vairagya – Dispassion, detachment, or renunciation.

Vivarjitah – Relinquished or abandoned.

www.ingramcontent.com/pod-product-compliance
Lightning Source LLC
LaVergne TN
LVHW091721190726
843493LV00001B/398